# The Tribe:

# Collector's Edition

# Screenplay

**Raymond Thompson**

CUMULUS PUBLISHING LIMITED

# Copyright

## Dedication

For all Tribe fans around the world.
And to those dedicated to building a better, more
sustainable world for successive generations to inhabit.

# INTRODUCTION

It is difficult to believe that almost 11 years have passed since I wrote my Tribe memoir, 'Keeping the Dream Alive', which was published in 2011.

Re-reading the last chapter, to refresh myself on what exactly was happening at that point in the journey of The Tribe, it was even more difficult to believe that I had written in the third person, given that all elements associated with the journey of The Tribe in reality represent my own personal journey throughout my entire life.

I think possibly the reason is down to the fact that where my professional career is concerned, I cannot believe my good fortune. It is rather like it has occurred to someone else, rather than myself.

In addition, I found it very difficult to write about myself. Especially due to the fact that by nature I am a private (and shy) individual.

At some point, I might do a 'Volume 2' follow up to 'Keeping the Dream Alive' with an in depth behind the scenes and details of what occurred in the intervening years since 2011.

Most notable has been the loss of my beloved father in 2012 and my sister in 2021. Which places a profound nuance on what I am always telling people about how difficult it is on my vineyard sipping on a glass of wine to ignore the whisper of mortality that inhabits every fading sunset.

The last chapter of 'Keeping the Dream Alive' focused mainly on my sabbatical and the recharging of my batteries on the vineyard. Which has always been a refuge and welcome contrast away from the pressures of the business world.

I love the aesthetic. The vineyard is extremely photogenic with spectacular 360-degree views. A sea of green fields and rows of vines with rolling hills and distant mountains all around.

The location is special in other ways too. The vineyard is located in a rural community with approximately 1500 local residents and it reflects almost a lifestyle of days gone by.

A community isolated from the noise and pace of cities or even towns where locals know one another and respect and protect their own space, as well as the same for their fellow inhabitants. But rather than any aloof lifestyle, without exception, everyone is always there for one another. When needed.

I often think of the region as being life at 4 miles an hour. Where one can slow down to the true speed of life. It is impossible to get tractor rage on a tractor.

And the day a traffic light is introduced in the roads surrounding the small village would be the day that modern civilisation and technology has caught up. I am sure it would cause an outrage, signifying not only a blot on the landscape, but the first step to have something alien invade the natural world and endanger all that is special about mother nature. As well as the small close community.

Back in 2011, after completing 'The Tribe' memoir, I was more than creatively burnt out. Not solely due to 'The Tribe' but having been in production solidly for over 15 years.

With Cloud 9 also trading globally and expanding faster than I ever envisaged, the pressure of burning the midnight oil 24/7 was catching up. I have often referred to it as a self-inflicted nervous breakdown.

This was all exacerbated having suffered from some disappointments and frustrations in Hollywood. So, I really did need to take some time out.

Rather than watching flowers grow, this was replaced by grapes. Along with gazing at the sun rising at dawn and setting against a spectacular backdrop of multi colours, heralding the dark sky which would then house a planetarium of stars, seemingly stretching from the small community accommodating the vineyard into far beyond. Infinity.

It was a strange feeling, taking time out. From travelling the world. Rushing to airports to catch flights. Having assistants constantly filling diaries. Organizing my time and life years in advance with back-to-back meetings and production schedules. So, it took some time to get used to taking time out, wakening up each and every day, wondering what I might do.

But due to business demands and my lifestyle, there was never any opportunity of doing nothing.

For those who have read 'Keeping the Dream Alive', they will no doubt recall the routine I outlined in the memoir and the context and reasons why my attempted sabbatical came into being back in 2011.

For the previous two years I had been in discussions regarding a potential motion picture and sequel to 'The Tribe'. And had signed with a major and very powerful Hollywood agency, CAA (Creative Arts Agency).

My agent was Jon Levin, who represented a number of 'A-list' clients, ranging from Brad Pitt to Will Smith, Jennifer Aniston to Arnold Schwarzenegger.

The agency also represented so many influential clients in the entertainment industry. Indeed CAA, along with UTA and WME (United Talent Agency and William Morris Endeavour) between them seemed to represent virtually every 'A-list' actor, actress, producer, director, and writer in the Film and Television industries.

Speaking of WME, I was also associated with an extremely talented (and lovely individual) ex-agent of WME, Alan Gasmar, who set up a boutique management company (Alan Gasmar and Friends). I was introduced to Alan through a shrewd and astute entertainment lawyer – Eric Feig, to whom I also warmed, as besides being capable on all matters legal, Eric is a true gentleman. And both Eric and Alan really believed in 'The Tribe' and were keen - along with my own agent - to try and bring either a motion picture or sequel to fruition.

This resulted in an introduction to Rob Cohen. Who is best known and loved as a director of the mega successful franchise 'Fast and Furious' but other iconic motion pictures as well, such as the Vin Diesel vehicle 'XXX', along with 'The Mummy'.

Rob's impressive track record also included time as an executive vice president of 'Motown's motion picture division', working in close association with the legendary Berry Gordy. So, Rob was certainly a veteran on both sides of the camera and had a unique insight of both creative and commercial elements.

Around the same time, Alan introduced me to one of his clients. A gifted young writer, Jason Rothenberg.

There were consequentially several meetings arranged throughout Hollywood with key studios and outlets whereby Rob, Jason and I discussed 'The Tribe'. And with Alan, Eric and Jon's assistance, we came very close in arriving at a framework to bring it all together.

But Hollywood has an interesting culture, which has evolved since the city of dreams became synonymous with the silver screen and Hollywood titans ruled studios with an iron fist. And velvet glove. Depending on how useful one might be.

These days, studios are still all powerful but now are mostly controlled by Wall Street.

Screenplays are assessed not only on their own merits and creative aspirations but the potential effects to fiscal bottom lines and fluctuating share prices. Hardly surprising given that the film and television business is after all a business and industry.

If one doesn't succumb to the studio system - or are willing to operate under that methodology - then the only option is to try and trade as an independent, which gives more creative freedom, but less of a commercial infrastructure.

Given that studios seem to control distribution around the world and even today have extended their operations into streaming platforms, independents still need to rely on some of the major studios in some way. And there is always a distinct difference between what is referred to as a 'studio picture' and an 'indie' one.

Throughout my career - even at the BBC – I never had to experience any of the requirements and constraints which seem normal within the Hollywood method of operating.

I enjoyed total creative freedom when I founded the Cloud 9 Screen Entertainment Group in 1994. Whereby I had editorial control and could pursue my creative visions unimpaired.

So, I certainly found it a very difficult transition to not really have a so called 'voice' on 'The Tribe'. And therefore, could not protect or police the creative integrity, which for me is always paramount.

Furthermore, I could not see the fan base being satisfied, for instance, with casting so called 'marquee names' to replace our current cast. All of whom are talented and gifted individuals.

It is always necessary to keep an open mind and to compromise wherever possible. But the creative process is such that it is impossible to have the proverbial horse become a camel. And I really did struggle with the direction at times on where 'The Tribe' might be taken, which was contrary to my own aspiration and creative vision.

The death blow though was the prospect of going into 'development hell'. Which is a term used for developing projects rather than producing them and bringing them to market.

So many titles take so long to come to fruition. In addition, many Hollywood so called 'A-listers' seem to have dozens of projects in development, which means just by the logistics that they are booked up several years ahead. Resulting in elongated periods of development.

As so often happens, once a project has been developed, a cast member may be available, but then the director is not.

Then if one waited until the director is available, then the cast might not be free.

If everything is aligned in terms of availabilities of the key members of the team and it all appears to be coming together on the surface, Hollywood has a term known as 'musical chairs' whereby executives either leave or are fired. In which case, so many projects fall by the wayside at the eleventh hour (or a million and eleventh, more like, with development hell) because the replacement executives often wish to focus more on their own pet projects. Rather than to inherit and support the ones instigated by their predecessors.

Another element is the cynical notion that 'you're only as good as your last movie'. Many key creatives are hot via box office success (or critical acclaim) but their leverage can dramatically alter or become severely diluted through poor box office performance.

There is also a risk averse mentality in television as well as the motion pictures industry. Resulting in so many pilots being made to market test. It is understandable, to be fair. Given the huge sums of investment required to fund a production.

In motion pictures, some of the so called 'stars" fees are really astronomical. It is no wonder that so many budgets exceed 100 million dollars and therefore studios are understandably very cautious regarding committing to investment.

So, the development process is rather like a double-check system. On the face of it that is. I think the longer something is in development seems to be conflated that it somehow is far less risky.

In my days of being a jobbing screenwriter (prior to founding Cloud 9), I used to be retained to do what is known as 'script doctoring', which is really rather like trying to polish or tighten or improve a screenplay.

On one occasion, a major producer threw a script at me (thankfully not his cigar) and asked me to give it a good going over. I asked him what in particular caused him concern and stared open mouthed in pure disbelief when he advised that he hadn't actually read it as yet.

It seems that there is a requirement to have a gazillion drafts, with possibly even several writers, which further elongates the development process. Rather like taking one step forward and a hundred back.

If you look at the credits of any motion picture, you will certainly see several writers on the credits.

I might be paranoid. My wife always says that if I went to a rugby game and saw the players in a huddle or scrum that I would be sure that they are criticising my script. There might be some credence to that comment, which isn't exactly flippant.

But confirmed by the fact that so many writers are brought in - along with script doctors - to undertake re-writes, which can be counterproductive. As well as slowing the development process down and stretching it to the very limit. Resulting in what should be a rewarding and fulfilling experience being reduced to a frustrating ordeal.

Imagine. A Hollywood executive might like one version of a screenplay, but a director prefers another version. A powerful cast member with clout might demand a totally different rewrite to enhance his or her own character. But this version might not be the preferred one of a distributor or investor or fellow cast member or director or Hollywood executive.

It is like a merry go round which results in a blur. Not an environment in which I wanted (or want) to operate. So, I decided to move on. Rob and Jason felt much about the same. As we simply could not find a consistent pathway with a third party who shared our direction.

Jason incidentally went on to become showrunner and executive producer of the highly successful 'The 100'. And Rob of course is always in demand as a director and continues to deliver excellent work.

Alan has evolved into a very successful producer in his own right and is best known for bringing the phenomenally successful 'Vikings' to our screen.

Eric has built his law firm into a vibrant enterprise and represents very major clients in our industry.

It is really great to see them all doing so well. And we remain in touch.

I decided to leave CAA agency and through another contact in Hollywood was introduced to key executives at Legendary. A major Hollywood studio, responsible for so many successful franchises. And I signed an option to develop a sequel, thinking that at long last I had found a home for 'The Tribe'.

I am bound by a non-disclosure agreement (NDA) and am unable to reveal too much detail. But it didn't work out at Legendary as I had hoped and expected.

I am still involved with my colleague. Who has a tremendous track record as a producer and is committed to 'The Tribe'. We have been developing a sequel and will never give up our efforts to bring the sequel to fruition.

But I would prefer that I am never in a position to have to write or produce anything I do not creatively believe in. It's not who I am. I would prefer that nothing happens rather than a creative works coming into existence that does not represent the creative aspirations or vision which I have.

It would not only dilute my own creative integrity but I think would be terribly unfair to our tribal fanbase and betray their loyalty and devotion.

'The Tribe' of course isn't the only title within Cloud 9's portfolio of product. Indeed, we have a substantial catalogue of other programming, along with music and other subsidiary business interests, from merchandising to publishing.

In addition, we operate an artisan and boutique distribution entity (Cumulus).

So, as much as I enjoyed indulging myself in the natural world and getting in tune with the joys of mother earth and nature back in 2011, the pressures of business remained constant and I had no option but to devote more and more time away from sitting on the tractor and pondering about the meaning of life over a glass (okay, I admit, several glasses) of fine wine.

This included overseeing digitising all our several hundred episodes of programming as well as coordinating various licensing arrangements with distributors and broadcasters around the world.

It is very humbling that our titles are regularly shown in so many countries, but the process does precipitate very complicated administration, ranging from legal matters to even promotion and PR elements. Including doing press interviews.

Time therefore takes on a totally different dimension. 'The Tribe' airs all over the world. Mostly streaming these days. But major terrestrial broadcasters are still intrigued with the title, such as 'SABC2' in South Africa who started broadcasting in 2022. It is all new for the journalists, but like 'Groundhog Day' given that the series was produced so many years ago, it feels like constant repetition talking about titles as if they are brand new.

Nevertheless, it goes along with what is necessary and required for our global audience to be able to view our product. The same applies to all our titles and isn't solely confined to 'The Tribe'.

I am often asked what my favourite title is. Which is rather like asking a parent who their favourite child is. In many ways, each and any element of the creative process is such that every element is special. It can't be otherwise. Given that a creative person has brought the creation into existence, which isn't exactly like giving birth, but almost (metaphorically).

I have to confess though that 'The Tribe' is extra special.

Coming of age in the 60's/70's, amidst a cultural and music revolution, I think especially resonates with me. Considering that 'The Tribe' is about building a better world from the ashes of the old. Whereby young people are in full control. And the future is entirely their's to create.

I have always been fascinated with this concept. Ever since I was in my early teens. Probably rebelling against authority and some of the older generation who screwed up (at least in my view at the time).

But as the years have passed I have become even more intrigued, given that I became 'older' and as a father was very concerned regarding what kind of world my children would inhabit.

Which became more punctuated when I became a grandfather, and I am heartened that so many liberties and freedoms and human rights are occurring. Such as the LGBT+ community. As well as an awareness of the need to protect our planet and to be in tune with climate change and all that entails. Along with the constant need to be aware of addressing just so many social injustices around the world.

I view 'The Tribe' as an allegorical tale in many ways. A 'Blue sky dystopia'. Where for all of the challenges and conflicts and dangers, out of all that despair, one aspect remains constant. Being hope.

It has been a real joy to have had the opportunity over the years since 'Keeping the Dream Alive' was published to work with A.J. Penn on 'The Tribe' tie-in novels. 'The Tribe: A New World' in 2011, 'The Tribe: A New Dawn' in 2014. 'The Tribe: (R)Evolution' in 2019.

A.J. is a pseudonym of a very gifted writer (for the record, contrary to any rumours – it is not me) and it is creatively important to me to be able to have the ongoing saga continue. And no need for this to stop, subject of course to supply and demand. As long as the fans have an appetite for more tribal stories, and I'm sure that A.J. and myself will be able to find some time to bring them to the marketplace.

It was also really great to be reunited with the cast through 'The Tribe' audiobooks.

I have long been a fan of radio drama. As well as the iconic broadcast of 'War of the Worlds'.

So rather than just have the cast read the novels as normally occurs with an audiobook, we interwove sound effects, as well as music, which became a mammoth task in post production terms.

The audiobooks have been successfully received, which is heartening. Like 'listening to' an episode. But of course, rather than an episode, it would take more than a day and a night to listen to all three audiobooks, given that each runs for about 12 hours.

Hardly surprising that over 40 hours (non-edited) was such a mammoth task to edit down to a comfortable running time.

Around the time of working on the storylines of 'The Tribe: (R)Evolution' (in 2018, prior to the book being written), we started considering the notion of doing a Tribe game.

I have to confess that I am a bit of a dinosaur regarding the gaming industry. But our team of developers believed that a preferred style would be 'Retro'. And in some consumer testing, this was certainly confirmed to be the case.

Being a relatively small independent company, we also couldn't raise a sufficient budget to compete with the 'Triple A' titles – some budgets are in excess of $100 million.

But nevertheless, the investment I made for the game was substantial (in relative terms of course).

We used the 'RPG Maker MV' software, which was excellent to accommodate the 'Retro' feel that we wanted. But equally, was a little restraining in some areas (it has to be said), preventing us from doing what we would have ideally liked to do.

I am very proud of the end result. I think that the artwork is stunning. I hope our players warm to the music, as well as the story and dialogue (which I actually did myself) and we tried to interweave all manner of quests and themes to keep a player's interest.

But above all, to provide a platform whereby the player could become a member of the tribe and interact.

Thankfully, the game has been very well received.

There have been a few negative comments though (thankfully minimal and in the minority), which is understandable if a player was expecting a gazillion dollar budget mega franchise type of multiplayer all-bells-and-whistles.

We really pushed the boundaries and did the best that we could do with the software and budget we had.

I am not against adding to this game if the market demands and hopefully widening the technical software capabilities to make the game more user friendly as we go along.

Other highlights include around 2015/2016, the extremely gifted actor Joseph Gordon-Levitt, through his 'Hitrecord' community, brought to our attention a young lady and a huge fan of 'The Tribe' in Germany who had an impossible dream to visit New Zealand.

This young lady has Asperger's syndrome (as indeed do I).

My wife and I founded the 'Cloud 9 Children's Foundation' several years ago to assist those touched by the autistic spectrum, (as well as other elements) but in the end, all that was required was encouragement and support to let the young lady realise that she must never give up on her dream. And, in line with the thematic of 'The Tribe' about keeping the dream alive, should never lose hope on her own dream.

In 2022, it was a real joy and pleasure to have the young lady finally arrive in New Zealand after so many years of struggle. Not only did she achieve her dream, but we were able to arrange a private lunch with her favourite cast member (Jennyfer Jewell, who played Ellie) as a highlight.

If the young lady didn't make it to New Zealand, I was planning to try and catch up with her in Germany to offer her support and encouragement. Given that she was also very keen to meet me in person.

I was planning to attend the MIPCOM television festival in Cannes in the south of France in 2019 to ease the mammoth workload associated with the distribution of our back catalogue and was hopeful that I could pursue some promising negotiations regarding 'The Tribe' and especially a possible association with a German company, 'Your Family Entertainment'. Which would have provided an opportunity of being in Germany, which would have ensured that I could also meet the young lady with the impossible dream.

But I just couldn't find space in the diary and decided to book a cruise in January 2020 to sail from Auckland to Sydney so that I could travel to Queensland and re-charge the batteries at my holiday home in Australia.

The plan was to stay for about 3 weeks.

Almost 3 years later, I am still here!

As everyone around the world sadly experienced, the whole world just seemed to close due to Covid, and my family and I decided to remain in Australia in lockdown. Borders were still open, but we did not relish staying in isolation in so called

'Covid hotels' whereby there was evidence that the virus spread and could not be contained. Rather like what occurred on cruise ships.

It is certainly ironic to have the world of fiction merge with the real world. The concept of 'The Tribe' seemed to become strangely prophetic. Especially given that young people appeared to be more immune. With the virus affecting more adversely older people especially.

We were inundated with messages from our fanbase. At both HQ and within our social media network moderation.

As a matter of routine, we always get a large number of messages. But the spike was significant. And very apparent that so many shared deep fear and worries about what might occur or how they will cope and where Covid might lead.

Concerns were not only confined to matters of health. But fiscal matters as well. With people unable to work, receive their pay checks and meet their monthly payment obligations. So many small businesses were suffering and going out of business of course. And even larger multi-national companies were commercially and fiscally vulnerable.

I decided to utilise the time to work on my creative endeavours, since any travel was non-existent, due to borders being closed and especially the constraints of isolation.

Consequently, I thought it might be appropriate to do a podcast with the cast. To share their thoughts on Covid, how they are coping.

Communication can often be so therapeutic and I hoped in expressing fears and vulnerabilities for mental wellbeing that any listener might feel a little more reassured. Realising that they are not alone and that there are coping strategies available which can be shared.

Or at the very least, if we were unable to allay any fears or provide reassurance, then the podcast might be an interesting way to take the listener off for an hour or two from their own predicaments.

It was certainly special to have the time and opportunity to speak with the cast. Not surprising, given that without exception, every single member of the cast are special individuals. As well as gifted and talented ones. Which was why they were cast in the first place.

We did not just want to hire their talent but wished for them to feel committed and invested into the themes of the series. There was no room for egos or disruptive and divisive behaviours.

All the cast and crew really were the ultimate professionals, and I am indebted to them, as without their hard work and special skills, 'The Tribe' wouldn't be the special series that it is today.

Not all members of the cast and crew have remained in the industry. Many have married and have become fathers and mothers and have pursued other career paths, rather than the entertainment industry. But all cast and crew still remain very close to one another, which is not surprising. 'The Tribe' in many ways is a tribe within a tribe. AKA, family.

For the cast and crew who have remained in the industry, I am equally as proud as I am of all our team to observe how careers have developed.

So many of our crew have gone on to do exceptional work, ranging from the Academy Award winning Dan Hennah (our production designer on 'The Tribe') who worked on 'Lord of the Rings' to Mike Hedges (our sound mixer) who has worked on so many tentpole franchises. Including 'Lord of the Rings' and also 'Avatar'.

Sir Richard Taylor of 'Weta Workshops' is also an Academy Award winner and remains a close friend, having worked closely on the early Cloud 9 productions.

And even one half of 'Flight of the Conchords' – being Jemaine Clement – started as an extra on 'The Tribe' alongside the enormously gifted Taika Waititi who also had a speaking part in our series of 'Revelations: The Initial Journey' (which was designed as a vehicle for the very gifted and lovely Tom Hern).

Tom and I incidentally have ongoing discussions about a Tribe movie. Tom is a very talented producer with a blossoming career and already tremendously successful track record, including the critically acclaimed and awesome motion picture 'The Dark Horse'. Which was directed by none other than our own tribal brother James Napier (who played Jay in 'The Tribe').

Another highlight since completing 'Keeping the Dream Alive' in 2011 has been enjoying both the company of James and Tom who visit the vineyard on occasion and it's never long enough to enjoy their company over dinner.

In true yin and yang fashion though, sadly, life isn't only about highlights. There has been pain as well as joy.

In 2021, my beloved sister had a fall. She lived in the UK, was taken to hospital where they ran some tests and discovered that rather than any injury associated with the fall, my sister actually had a brain tumour which was terminal and was only given 6 months to live.

This was extremely difficult with borders being closed and I had to rely on Zoom for communications with my sister and other family members in the UK. I was not even able to travel to attend her funeral. But of course was there - as I always will be - in spirit.

My sister and I were close. Very close. I mentioned to her during our Zoom calls as her strength ebbed and the very cruel disease slowly spread, that with the time zone differences, that I would look at the moon and connect with her, knowing that if she looked at the moon in her own time zone that we would be seeing the same element of the natural world. So, there was no need to get frustrated as even talking became a major challenge and exhausted her.

I still think of her. Every time I look at the moon. We are all interconnected as much as the earth, sky, and sea. But also, by the powerful emotions and feelings. AKA known as love.

Love is truly eternal. Even if life in this incarnation is not. But love does transcend death I believe.

I still have a sister (as well as a mother, father, and younger brother – all of whom have passed away - and they will walk with me forever). And we still have a relationship. But simply in a different incarnation.

It has been a difficult time. Having the pain of two bereavements concerning my father and sister. But this has been contrasted with much joy and I feel truly blessed.

As per the beginnings of the 'Keeping the Dream Alive' memoir, I am sitting in my holiday home in Queensland gazing out at a tropical landscape of palm trees. And yes, there are kangaroos lazing and grazing in the morning sun.

Though the one I was convinced mimicked me during my workout in my memoir seems to have moved elsewhere (presumably not to a gym!).

As well as fans of 'The Tribe', I was very touched and humbled to know that many who read 'Keeping the Dream Alive' found it to be an interesting behind the scenes record of the Film and Television industry, along with the formation and evolution of the Cloud 9 Screen Entertainment Group.

I have kept myself very busy writing and composing. It is something I just need to do and am compelled to do for some reason. And have been writing several screenplays in order to chase some unfulfilled creative dreams in the motion picture arena (but within an indie methodology as opposed to a Hollywood studio one).

Possibly although Hollywood really isn't for me, in reality, I am not for Hollywood in the same way. So, I might be part of the problem. As much as I need to be involved in the business aspects of our industry, at the core, I am a writer (and composer).

In the cold light of dawn, when everyone else sleeps, a writer writes. And I know of no writer who does not nestle in bed with heartache and sorrow more often than not.

Filling blank pages is a nightmare at times for me. A sort of love/hate situation. As much as I feel compelled to do it, I also try and avoid it. But eventually just can't help myself from gazing at the blank page and forcing myself to make a start.

It is very motivating to see that my close friend and colleague Harry Duffin also continues to write. If any fans haven't done so already, they should check out 'Chicago May' and 'Jail Tails' as well as Harry's fabulous adaptation of 'The Tribe' tie-in novel, 'Birth of the Mall Rats'.

I have in fact just read Harry's latest novel, 'Island of Dreams', which is a fantastic read and highly recommended (it's due to be published around December 2022 but might filter into January 2023 by the time it reaches other platforms).

Back to my own writing. I have been forever asked to publish a version of 'The Tribe' as a screenplay. And decided that now is the time, given that I have hinted that I would do so on many occasions and have rightly been picked up on it why it has not been actioned.

Part of the reason was that I have many versions of 'The Tribe' in screenplay form. Which is normal in the development process. But I have chosen this version to be published as it best illustrates the closest of what I would aspire to have as a motion picture version (the television sequels of course would be totally different).

Also, this version interweaves Flame and The Privileged tribe. How I originally wanted them to be portrayed, but due to editorial constraints and compliance for broadcasting within the children's realms of programming, I could not utilise this portrayal in 'The New Tomorrow'.

As stated in 'Keeping the Dream Alive' I am still proud of 'The New Tomorrow' and think the cast and crew did a fabulous job. My point is that it all evolved into a much younger version than originally planned. And there is nothing at all wrong with that. The series works and stands alone on its own merit.

Another element of why I chose this version of the screenplay is the difficulty in working to a brief. Many distributors and studios required a so called 'origin story' to allay their concerns that realistically, given that 'The Tribe' series is 'cult' and not a mainstream franchise, the majority of a new audience would really need to be introduced to each character in the setup.

I think this is a valid concern. So, I went back to the original blueprint to try and remain truthful to the original continuity of what occurred in the original series, but also to try and tell the same story in a slightly different way (especially for fans familiar with the series).

My hope and aspiration was to arrive at a version that would appeal to the existing fanbase (with intriguing elements such as Flame and possibly a slightly different take on a similar setup and character framework and interplay) along with an origin type of story that would introduce those unfamiliar with 'The Tribe' into who/why/where/what.

It is certainly not a so called 'shooting script'. But a works in progress. And I continue to polish and develop, along with working on some other versions. But at least it can serve as almost a collector's limited edition, for those keen on experiencing behind the scenes elements and trivia associated with 'The Tribe'.

We do have lots of other material which we might publish in the future. Including style guides. Costume and makeup designs. All manner of trivia and material which might be of interest to those as a collectable.

I will certainly be discussing future storylines with A.J. and examining potentially expanding the game, as well as considering doing a 'Volume 2' of 'Keeping the Dream Alive'.

But in addition to running the Cloud 9 group of companies and distributing our back catalogue, I am busy developing a portfolio of product and at the top of the list certainly is still a 'Tribe' sequel.

I cannot promise that it will come to fruition. I can promise that if it does not, then it will not be for the want of trying.

I hope you enjoy reading the screenplay.

And at least the opportunity of having a bit of a catch up on what has been occurring over the past years since the publication of 'Keeping the Dream Alive' in 2011.

As always, it means a great deal to all our cast and crew as well as myself. Especially to have your loyalty and support over all these years. It is always very humbling and touching.

So, thank you for being there for us.

And above all, no matter what obstacle or challenge in your lives, always keep your dream alive.

Much love to you all.

Raymond Thompson MNZM.

December 2022.

Raymond Thompson

THE TRIBE


Written

by

RAYMOND THOMPSON

(Inspired by the cult television series,
The Tribe)

Raymond Thompson

FADE IN

EXT. DESERTED STREET. DAY.

Graffiti on the walls, tagging, featuring stylized street art portraying 'Locos Rule'.

Smoldering vehicles. Looted buildings. A newspaper (like tumbleweed) blowing.

The fading, charred headline announcing that the global Pandemic is reaching unprecedented proportions.

A cow ambling around, looking for a place amidst all the concrete to graze in the ghostly, deserted streets. Hints that nature is reclaiming the city with stems and veins of plants climbing walls, roots of trees cracking foundations.

And we pick up a feral and filthy looking URCHIN of a child as he raises a primitive bow, inserts an arrow from a quiver and takes aim.

> BRAY'S VOICE
> The world began without the
> human race ...

EXT. ROOFTOP. SKYSCRAPER. DAY.

BRAY, stealthily crossing the rooftop.

Once a gamer, into Manga, all things Japanese (Shinto, the code of Bushido which inspired so many of the online games he once played), he is VERY 'Zen', enigmatic, accomplished in martial arts, exudes a quiet confidence, relates to the elemental rather than the material, considering himself an eco-warrior. And has also clearly been influenced by nature. With braided flaxen plants intertwined with feathers as hair extensions.

Now he has reached the edge of the rooftop and is gazing across the environs of the deserted city.

> BRAY'S VOICE
> And I'm beginning to think
> it will end up pretty much
> the same way...

EXT. DESERTED STREETS. DAY.

Whoosh! An arrow soars through the air – grazing the cow – and embeds itself in a tree. The cow runs off. The URCHIN lowers his bow despondently.

A SATELLITE

circling MOTHER EARTH with news 'CHATTER'.

Something of a significant magnitude is happening worldwide. A myriad of VOICES in various languages - through which we hear snippets of English.

                    VOICES
          The   Security   Council   is
          meeting   again   in   closed
          emergency session. Meanwhile
          segments  of  the  population
          are being tested to identify
          those  likely  to  be  more  at
          risk.

EXT. EVACUATION CAMP. DAY.

A long line of CHILDREN and YOUNG PEOPLE, featuring a slightly younger yet to be introduced ZOOT, queuing to be examined by OFFICIALS sitting behind desks.

The  OFFICIALS  are  all  wearing  germ-protective masks. Some are taking blood samples,   temperatures,   examining   the children.  Others  are  stamping  papers: CONTAMINATED, UNCONTAMINATED.

ZOOT  has  arrived  at  the  desk,  gazes contemptuously  at  the  OFFICIALS,  then suddenly lunges, yanks off the mask of one OFFICIAL, grabs the stamp from the OFFICIAL's  hand  -  and  drives  it  into the  OFFICIAL'S  forehead,  branding  him CONTAMINATED.

SECURITY converge.

ZOOT leaps on the desk and screams in a manic intensity as he addresses the young people in the long queue.

> ZOOT
> Rise up! Take control!

INT. SEALED CHAMBER. DAY

SCIENTISTS looking almost sinister, futuristic, not of this world in protective hooded masks and decontamination suits examining test tubes.

> BRAY'S VOICE
> For a while we all thought
> it was just a virus. Which
> mutated. Yeah, right! But
> that was just lies. A cover
> up. By the governments of
> the world. Or was it?

EXT/INT. HOSPITAL. DAY.

Pandemonium, OVERCROWDING,panic. SECURITY and RECEPTIONISTS unable to cope with the volume and swell of desperate, frightened PEOPLE and we hear an assortment of fragmented VOICES begging, pleading.

>               ASSORTMENT OF VOICES
>                    (OVERLAP)
>          Please, I've GOT to see a
>          doctor! C'mon, we've been
>          waiting for over three
>          hours! Where else can we
>          get vaccinated! If all
>          the doctors and nurses
>          are so busy, what about
>          the vaccine? Give me the
>          vaccine and I'll godamn
>          vaccinate myself! I've got
>          a temperature! I need to
>          see a  doctor - NOW!

>               BRAY'S VOICE
>          Whatever it was, one thing
>          for sure, there was really
>          no cure - or hope. For all
>          the adults, especially.

EXT. CEMETERY. DAY.

A slightly younger yet to be introduced
AMBER, distraught, placing flowers on the
graves of her parents, recently deceased.

And as the camera cranes back, we can see
that the cemetary is packed with many new
services being simultaneously conducted
- bereavement occurring on a mammoth
scale.

INT. HOUSE. DAY.

A FAMILY hugging, clinging to each other, saying their heartbreaking goodbye, KIDS, PARENTS, sobbing, as they watch a news ANCHOR on television.

> ANCHOR
> Authorities are appealing
> for calm throughout the
> evacuation process.
> Priority will be given to
> those aged under 18 years
> old with a certificate of
> being uncontaminated.

MONTAGE - SPLIT SCREEN

Packed airports, train stations, panic, chaos. PEOPLE scrambling and fighting to get on trains, through the departure gates of airlines.

> BRAY'S VOICE
> Maybe it was a scientific
> experiment gone disastrously
> wrong. Some people even
> thought it was all down to
> genetic engineering. Or
> bacterial warfare. That's
> the problem. When you don't
> know who - or what - to
> believe any more.

One MAN breaking the line to get even a few feet ahead is shot - dead - by a frustrated ZOOT who starts to fire in a frenzy, screaming above all the panic.

> ZOOT
> Power and Chaos! Power and Chaos!! Power and Chaos!!!

The fading resemblance of any order is gone. SECURITY GUARDS, unable to control the panicked stampede, dive for cover and return fire as ZOOT grabs human shields and backs away, still firing but now laughing manically.

> BRAY'S VOICE
> Or was it just anger that pushed us all over the edge into this crazy world of madness we live in now these days?

MULTIPLE FRAGMENTED IMAGES (LIKE THE SCREEN IS SHATTERING)

A mass exodus of PEOPLE leaving towns, cities. Trails of REFUGEES on foot, traffic jams on the freeway, panicked FACES, scared CHILDREN, yelling, screaming, gridlock. Shattered, fragmented images as if society is breaking up, Mother Earth dying.

EXT. SUBURBIA. DAY.

Sinister looking security VEHICLES with tinted glass (so that the occupants are obscured) patrolling deserted streets. An ominous voice blaring through a loudspeaker.

> VOICE
> (distort)
> Code one. Isolation now in effect.

> BRAY'S VOICE
> Is it really the end? Or just the beginning?

EXT. DESERTED CITY. DAY.

BRAY, on the rooftop of the skyscraper, tenses at the os distant sound of a pulsing siren (from an unseen police patrol car) and crouches for cover.

> BRAY'S VOICE
> The only question is... the beginning of what? The end?

EXT. CITY. DESERTED STREETS. DAY.

The URCHIN seen earlier hunting is now running through the empty, ghostly streets. Flat out. Whimpering. Absolutely terror-stricken. Stealing petrified looks behind. As the distant os sound of the siren is becoming louder, louder.

The URCHIN is being chased by a wild, menacing, threatening looking Loco security PATROL who speed after him on roller blades.

The URCHIN is a STRAY. Those not members - or under the protection - of a Tribe. Dangerous. Banishment from a Tribe is like a death sentence. So hard to fend for oneself in these, the cities of children, let alone in the suburbs or deserted surrounding countryside now inhabited by only the young.

The Loco PATROL finally catch up to the stray, hurl him, spread-eagled against a wall - and search him.

A RECONNAISSANCE RAT PATROL

Suddenly appearing out of nowhere (an alley way actually) converging, ambushing the LOCOS.

They are led by the leader - AMBER. We saw her in the cemetery earlier. Now she looks very funky, with an attitude as attractive and unique as the tight Zulu knots in her hair, her expressive make-up and grungy sense of individualist fashion punctuating that she rarely follows a trend - but sets it.

Another RAT in this patrol is the sensuous and spiritual Tribe philosopher and medicine woman - EDEN. And like AMBER, also clearly a capable warrior.

After exchanging a few impressive blows, the LOCO patrol quickly realize that they won't survive long mixing it with the RATS - especially when AMBER spins and kicks in a spectacular martial arts movement - and they scatter.

                    AMBER
          You ok? (the Stray nods)
          What's your name?

                    STRAY
          Sammy.

                    EDEN
          What are you doing? In the
          Loco sector?!

                    SAMMY
          Looking for something to
          eat.

                    AMBER
          Oh, and they figured you're
          an assassin trying to 'take
          out' Zoot, I suppose!

SAMMY is not smiling. AMBER gently dabs at blood trickling from the STRAY'S mouth.

                    AMBER
          Have you always been a
          stray? (he nods) Never been
          a member of any Tribe? -


                    EDEN
            (knowing where this is
                    leading)
          Amber!


                    AMBER
          We can't just leave him.
          Look at him. He has no hope
          of surviving on the streets.
          No way. Not with Zoot about
          to make an 'appearance'.
          (to the others) Come on.
          Let's go. Better make a
          move. While we can!


ON THE ROOFTOP OF THE SKYSCRAPER

BRAY moves closer to the edge of the
rooftop and gazes down at the city square
below.

IN THE MAIN CITY SQUARE

A crack of deafening, almost unbearable
noise. The os sound of a police patrol
car approaching ... closer ... CLOSER.

The LOCO TRIBE are assembled, lining the
streets. It is an awesome sight. War paint

streaking their faces, wild dreadlocks, scavenged clothes. They look feral. All now ululating in a frenzied shrieking.

And the legendary warrior ZOOT protruding from a modified graffiti-covered police patrol car, accompanied by his second in command, the GUARDIAN, along with the MILITIA of the Loco republican guard roller blading beside the car, arrives.

We can recognize ZOOT, having seen him earlier from the dreadlocks, but now in this incarnation he is streaked with war paint and looks like a renegade Native American Indian, partly dressed in furs and feathers, but also a punk styled (pinned) police officer's uniform and military hat and goggles.

Behind the car a long line of ravaged STRAYS are following, their wrists bound, tethered to long ropes.

This is still a world of no Internet, power, and VERY primitive in many ways, but some - the powerful - such as Zoot - have traded gas to fuel the very few vehicles commandeered or scavenged.

FEATURING BRAY

furtively watching, listening to ZOOT addressing the assembly with more than hints of a manic, zealot conviction.

                    ZOOT
          Loco brothers and sisters,
          check out these strays. They
          should have joined a Tribe
          like the Locos, right? Then
          they wouldn't be condemned!?
          But protected! Let me hear
          the word of Zoot now!

He thrusts his arms aloft, crosses his
wrists to cue his 'word', his motto. All
respond in unison, chanting, whipped into
a frenzy.

                 THE LOCO TRIBE
          Power and Chaos! Power and
          Chaos!! Power and Chaos!!!

                 BRAY'S VOICE
          At times I wonder for those
          of us still living - if
          we're actually dead in
          reality. Like all the rest.
          And have gone to hell.

INT. LOOTED SHOPPING MALL. DAY.

Now a fortress citadel (and home of the
Mall Rats).

In the main centre square, LEX is playing
basketball with some other members of
the RATS. He has rugged good looks, an
abrasive charm, and is clearly very

athletic as he slam dunks the ball into
the net. With ease.

AMBER, EDEN, SAMMY and the reconnaissance
PATROL seen earlier in the city arrive,
AMBER not at all pleased.

                    AMBER
          Good to see the place has
          been cleaned up, Lex!

It has not. It's a mess. Clothes, garbage
litter the area. LEX bounces, dribbles
the ball past some other PLAYERS.

                    LEX
          Back off. We're just taking
          a break. I'll make sure it
          all gets done.

                    AMBER
          You've been saying that all
          week.

                    LEX.
          Have I ever let you down?

                    AMBER
          Constantly.

He pops another ball into the net then
turns and glares, noticing SAMMY.

                    LEX
        What the hell is ... that?!


                   AMBER
        Think you mean "Who", Lex.
        Everyone ... this is Sammy!

The other RATS nod and one who was playing
basketball, SALENE, crosses to SAMMY and
they touch fists as a greeting.


                  SALENE
        Hey, Sammy ... Salene.

But LEX just still glares coldly at a
very uneasy SAMMY.


                    LEX
        Strays aren't welcome here,
        Amber!


                   AMBER
        Yeah, well, you're not
        exactly making Sammy feel
        right at home now, are
        you?!


                   EDEN
        Give him a break, Lex. He's
        only young -

                    LEX
Still a stray. No way this
Mall is gonna turn out to
be a home for losers!


                   AMBER
That's rich. Coming from
you!


                    LEX
I earned the right to be
here. Just as much as you,
Amber. Or anyone else.
Thought we agreed anyone
joins ONLY by initiation -


                   AMBER
No-one said anything about
strays joining the Tribe,
Lex. Sammy's only being
given a safe haven. For
the time being. And you'd
better get used to it. We
might have someone else
arriving later tonight.


EXT. SUBURBIA. DAY.

BRAY skateboards through a deserted
and decaying part of once middle class
suburbia.

From an eerie SUBJECTIVE camera it is as
if he is being watched, almost stalked,

by something, someone.

BRAY senses it, glances around uneasily.

ANOTHER STREET

As BRAY rounds a corner he notices – a ROOSTER PATROL ahead, on motocross bikes each side of a slowly approaching car but souped up, modified, covered in graffiti.

BRAY stops. And comes face to face with the menacing PATROL.

> PATROL LEADER
> You're trespassing. The Roosters own this sector!

> BRAY
> Since when? Thought this sector was still open?

> PATROL LEADER
> Since any time The Roosters like! And we don't need no permission from any stray.

FEATURING THE SUBJECTIVE CAMERA

Moving in CLOSER ... then stopping .... CLOSER then stopping.

                    BRAY
        I'm no stray. I just don't
        belong to a Tribe.


                    PATROL LEADER
        That makes you a stray in
        my book, Dude!


                    BRAY
        Look, I don't want any
        trouble.


                    PATROL LEADER
        Oh, you got trouble alright.
        Unless you got something of
        value to trade.


                    BRAY
        Like what?


                    PATROL LEADER
        Your life.


                    BRAY
        Oh, and how could that be?
        With only ten of you ...
        and one of me?


The LEADER scoffs disdainfully, indicates.
Two members of the PATROL lunge - but are
very quickly taken out with ease by BRAY
who leaps and twirls with spectacular
martial art kicks - like the expert he

is - as they try to seize him.

REVEALING A TIGER

Amidst a deafening roar - moving in for the kill.

The ROOSTERS scatter in all directions, the motocross bikes hurling away.

BRAY leaps on the roof of the car, desperately clinging as it accelerates, swerves, tires SCREECHING in a huge CLOUD of burning rubber.

With the TIGER in pursuit - and gaining fast.

A YARD

The car skids out of control, clips a tree, overturning on its side, hurling BRAY who lands, rolls for cover - and his life - as the TIGER passes, leaps in full flight onto the overturned car, pawing through the broken glass, feasting on the screaming, hysterical OCCUPANTS -

While BRAY makes his narrow escape.

INT. LOOTED HOUSE. SUBURBIA. DAY.

It is difficult for a clearly pregnant TRUDY as she looks at a torn photograph of her parents, sadly recalling the last days of being together.

TRUDY is attractive but a bit dipsy in a humorous and endearing way.

Now she has a twinge of pain. As BRAY arrives. And she notices that he is bruised, bleeding slightly.

> TRUDY
> What happened?!

> BRAY
> No time to explain. You all packed?

> TRUDY
> Couldn't find much.
> Everything has pretty much been looted.

> BRAY
> I did warn you.

BRAY wipes at his cuts as TRUDY jams the photograph with some items into a case. And she has another twinge of pain.

> BRAY
> What about you?- You ok?

> TRUDY
> Think so ... all we need is for me to go into labour - here.

                    BRAY
        We can stay if you prefer,
        Trudy.


                    TRUDY
        No. I don't want to stay. I
        don't want to have the baby
        here, Bray.


                    BRAY
        Then try and rest up. We'll
        have a better chance of
        getting to the city through
        all the sectors if we leave
        at nightfall. It's safer
        that way.


INT. ZOOT'S HEADQUARTERS. CITY HALL. DAY.

A SLAVE trader and his SECURITY are
examining the STRAYS seen earlier.


                    TRADER
        I'll have this one ... and
        her ... Don't know if I'll
        take him though - looks
        like he's dying.


                    ZOOT
        That's not the deal. You
        take them all. If they die
        - that's not my problem!


He indicates to the GUARDIAN and he nods

to Loco GUARDS who steady the STRAYS who
scream in agony as they are branded 'L'
from a white hot iron removed from a
garbage tin containing flaming coals.

> TRADER
> Gimmee a break, Zoot. Dead
> slaves are worthless.

> ZOOT
> So are dead traders.

He examines crates of vegetables and
other produce.

> ZOOT
> Could be a real problem if
> anything happened to you
> and it cut off any of my
> supplies. Imagine. If we
> don't do any more business
> and I don't protect you
> - who knows? You could
> even end up being branded
> yourself!

He smiles but it's ice-cold, enjoying the
reaction of the TRADER.

> ZOOT
> What's the matter? Don't
> fancy it? It's nothing.
> Only a bit of pain. Look!
> Might even enjoy it. Like

                    ZOOT (cont'd)
          me. But maybe that's
          because I'm a Loco.

He puts on an asbestos glove, grabs the
branding iron. The GUARDIAN and the Loco
SECURITY whoop it up as ZOOT presses the
iron - into his own cheek.

ZOOT doesn't even flinch, but amidst the
pain manages a grin as the steam sears
from his face and we can see a smouldering
'L' visible.

                         ZOOT
          Never try and negotiate
          with me! Remember. These
          slaves are only on loan.
          They belong to me. And the
          Locos. And so do you!

The TRADER nods.

                         ZOOT
          In case you forget .... (to
          the guards) Better steady
          your man. Do it!

They consider ZOOT, then take the TRADER'S
arms to steady him and he screams in
agony as ZOOT plunges the iron into the
TRADER'S cheek with more than a hint of
manic contempt.

                    ZOOT
          The Locos control all the
          power and chaos. And I make
          the rules.- And here's a
          new one for you. Don't ever
          question me again!

EXT. MOUNTAINS. DAY.

TRAVELLING over a photogenic mountainous
region -

TO REVEAL FLAME

on the VERY top of a snow-capped peak,
overlooking a breathtaking panorama.

And it is a surreal sight. The charismatic
leader of the Privileged, playing amazing
guitar licks like the virtuoso he is.

The ultimate guitar hero. Long blond hair
blowing in the wind as he head bangs,
trance-like. Amidst deafening, whistling
feedback and the most awesome, wailing
electric guitar licks anyone has ever
heard, reverberating seemingly around
all the lands.

FLAME is high maintenance, temperamental,
forever petulant, even bitchy - and we
could be forgiven for asking if he is
androgynous. Male? Or female? He sure
is striking looking. Even beautiful. The
ultimate rock star God.

EXT. FIELDS. PINE FOREST. MOUNTAINS. DAY.

The DISCARDS, the peasant slaves of the
Privileged, work the land.

Still the music and feedback reverberates
around and around.

In the far distance FLAME is visible,
rays of sun protruding over the crest of
the mountain top behind him, enshrining
him in a way, and he almost LOOKS like a
god, high in the heavens.

The DISCARDS are all in chains. Planting.
Tending crops. And unlike their masters
and mistresses - all are noticeably
overweight, unattractive with bar codes
tattooed in their arms.

BACK ON THE MOUNTAIN

Flame's deputy, HARMONY, along with her
SECURITY, watch FLAME continuing to
head bang as if in a trance, his fingers
bleeding as he moves across the frets and
bends the strings, WAILING more amazing
riffs.

HARMONY is absolutely gorgeous, long
braided hair, a lightning bolt tattooed
across one cheek. But she is also
insidious, scheming, calculating, the
real power behind the throne.

Right now she indicates FLAME to the
towering bodyguard, OX.

                    HARMONY
          Better get him down. He's
          had more than enough time.

FEATURING FLAME

Noticing OX and the SECURITY approach.
Then he suddenly -turns, runs - and leaps
from the mountain.

And could it be that he is ACTUALLY
FLYING?

THE PEASANT DISCARDS

Gaze up at FLAME in free fall in the
distance, twisting and turning upside
down - and all the while still clutching
his guitar and trying to play.

FLAME

Is suddenly yanked by the vine/rope around
one leg (like a bungee jump) and whoops it
up and starts to laugh manically amidst
all the FEEDBACK as he is catapulted,
hurled back up - and he loses grip of -

THE GUITAR

Which twists, falls through the air,
landing near -

AN ASTONISHED DISCARD SLAVE GIRL

Who crosses to the guitar, lifts it, overwhelmed – and overcome with emotion as she gives the instrument a huge ecstatic hug.

EXT. CITY STREETS. NIGHT.

BRAY and TRUDY travelling stealthily through the dark and deserted city streets, taking cover.

And narrowly avoiding danger when a Loco night PATROL passes with some Demon Dog PRISONERS, being led, shackled by rope, chains.

INT. SHOPPING MALL. NIGHT.

We are in a looted toy store. But it feels more like a cathedral from the dark ages – a nightmarish image, the candles illuminating toys on shelves with flickering light in a grotesque way.

Along with photographs of adults – parents, teachers, members of families who have gone before – set out along the shelves as if in a shrine.

Most of the younger members of the RATS are kneeling before the shrines, hands clasped, saying their bedtime prayers.

But MOUSE is driving EDEN nuts, refusing to get to bed. She is tiny, about 7 years old, a miniature box of dynamite, a real handful, jumping on her bed as if it is a trampoline.

>                    EDEN
>          That's enough, Mouse!

>                    MOUSE
>          I'm not tired.

>                    EDEN
>          Well, I am. Come on. All
>          of you. It's way past your
>          bedtime.

SAMMY is already in a bunk bed, the other young RATS featuring MOUSE climb into their beds - and EDEN tucks them in.

>                    MOUSE
>          I'm scared, Eden?!

>                    EDEN
>          Of what?

>                    MOUSE
>          If the Locos come. And
>          capture us all!

>                    EDEN
>          The Mall's well guarded,

                    EDEN (cont'd)
          Mouse. You know that.
          Remember. Fear makes the
          wolf bigger.


                    MOUSE
          Wolf?! What wolf?!!!


                    EDEN
          Settle down. It's just a
          saying.


                    MOUSE
          The Locos aren't though.
          They're real. And they
          might even try and eat us!

SAMMY cringes at the thought and some of
the younger RATS hide under blankets.


                    EDEN
          What?! The Locos would
          never do that -


                    MOUSE
          Lex said they might!


                    EDEN
          Yes, well Lex says a lot
          of things and sometimes it
          might pay you to try and
          not listen. And I suppose

                    EDEN (cont'd)
        'Lex' was going to protect
        you?


                    MOUSE
        If I do his laundry.


                    EDEN
        How could he? Honestly. You
        should have told me. Or
        Amber.


                    MOUSE
        Will you tell us a story?
        Might help get those mean
        Locos off my mind.


                    EDEN
        It's late.


                    MOUSE
        P-l-e-a-s-e!


                    EDEN
        You're something else, you
        really are. Ok, a quick
        story. Ready, everyone?

MOUSE and the younger RATS nod, settle in
their beds.

                    EDEN
          Once upon a time there was
          a little girl called Mouse
          (Mouse likes this). And
          one day, she and all her
          other friends - met a NEW
          friend. And his name was
          Sammy (he likes this, too)
          ...

IN THE FOOD HALL

Low level generators are causing flickering
light. AMBER and SALENE are trying to
prepare something to eat. AMBER sighs,
frustrated as the light dims way down low
casting looming shadows.

                    AMBER
          You're going to have to get
          your team to try and sort
          those generators out, Jack.
          I can hardly see a thing!

JACK and DAL, two members of the Tribe
not seen before, are sitting with LEX and
a few other RATS nearby. Apart from LEX,
most are in role playing dress up mode.

DAL is wearing a Darth Vader costume, long
black cloak, helmet, some are wearing
other masks, JACK is in a decontamination
suit, hood, and all look a little weird.

                    JACK
          (muffled under the hood)
     We'll get onto it. After we
     finish up this game. Won't
     be long.


                    LEX
     Don't know what the rush
     is. Soon the whole godamn
     world will be in darkness.
     And no generator will ever
     handle that. So we'd all
     better get used to it.


                    AMBER
     Well, that's a positive
     thought to end the day
     isn't it, Lex?


                    LEX
     True though.


                    AMBER
     Not if I can help it.

EXT. LOOTED SHOPPING MALL. NIGHT.

The top of a man hole cover is pried open
with a metal lever.

INT. FOOD HALL. LOOTED SHOPPING MALL.
NIGHT.

AMBER and SALENE continue to prepare food

and watch the role playing RATS with a degree of amusement.

DAL deals some home made cards. LEX checks them out, rolls the dice. Four.

> LEX
> So ... what do I do now?

> JACK
> You move four spaces, then pick up another card. See what skill level you've got up to.- Wait. I said four spaces, Lex. You're just on the line. That could be three. Or Five.

LEX does this but isn't too thrilled with it all.

> LEX
> What's with you? Everything has always got to be so precise.

> JACK
> It's all about being efficient, Lex.

> LEX
> No. It's all about being a nerd.

INT. SEWER. SHOPPING MALL. NIGHT.

FOOTSTEPS climbing down the run of a metal ladder into a sewer.

INT. FOOD HALL. LOOTED SHOPPING MALL. NIGHT.

The role playing RATS.

> JACK
> So ... who are you going to join? The Scientists doing genetic experiments? Or Dark Side Black unleashing bacterial warfare? Or the government covering up that it was just a virus that mutated?

> LEX
> How about a Mall Rat bored out of his mind?

> JACK
> Not my fault we have no Internet or online gaming, Lex. And it's the best I can do. If you don't like it - you don't have to play it!

                    LEX
        I LIVE it. Why the hell
        would I want to play it -

                    JACK
        Yeah, well, maybe we'd ALL
        enjoy the game a whole lot
        more if you didn't cheat!

LEX looks at JACK.

                    JACK
        Ah, thought I wouldn't
        notice, eh? I saw you slip
        that extra card into your
        pocket!

INT. SEWER. SHOPPING MALL. NIGHT.

A real RAT scurries past and we see the
beam of a flashlight cutting through the
darkness outlining approaching FIGURES.

INT. SHOPPING MALL. NIGHT.

JACK suddenly swallows nervously as LEX
stands.

                    LEX
        No-one accuses me of
        cheating. Ever. Even if I
        AM cheating.

                    JACK
        That makes no sense at all.

He cringes as LEX clenches a fist.

                    JACK
        Ok, Ok, it DOES make sense.

                    AMBER
        That's enough, Lex!

                    LEX
        Old Lexy boy is such a
        cool guy. And I reckon
        you'd better make a case
        of just how cool I am. If
        you know what's good for
        you. Cheating can have its
        advantages.

                    AMBER
        You've got a real weird way
        of looking at things at
        times, Lex.

                    LEX
        Who's saved everyone more
        than once by being foxy?
        Me! I wouldn't call that
        'weird'. And I deserve some
        respect!

EDEN arrives.

                    EDEN
What's going on?!


                    AMBER
Normal! Alpha male Lex
marking  his territory to
show everyone how 'tough'
he is.


                    LEX
Hold on a minute. Don't
blame me. Not my fault!


                    SALENE
Yes, it was, Lex.


                    AMBER
If it isn't one thing, it's
another. And I'm sick of
it. Constant bickering -


                    JACK
Technically it wasn't
bickering, Amber. I was
just accusing Lex of
cheating and ended up being
threatened -


                    AMBER
Give me a break! We should
be focusing on more
important matters.

                    AMBER (cont'd)
          Not wasting time playing
          games, arguing. There's no
          future in that.

                    LEX
          No future in anything. Not
          anymore. In case you've
          'forgotten'? We're on our
          own.

An ALARM.

                    JACK
          Doesn't sound like it!

Battle stations. Panic. Tension. AMBER
sighs to herself as EDEN, DAL, JACK,
SALENE spring into action to obtain
weapons of clubs, poles. LEX organizing
the MILITIA who converge.

                    LEX
          Seal off the main area.
          Move it!

IN THE MAIN AREA.

Hands pulling levers. Gates hurling down.

The younger RATS, featuring MOUSE
sprinting into the area, clinging to
the older RATS for protection, who also
arrive, followed by AMBER.

>                    MOUSE
>          Who is it?! The Locos?!!!

AMBER trying somehow to calm everyone down.

>                    AMBER
>          It isn't the Locos. I KNOW
>          who it is, Ok? So relax.
>          Everyone.

Relief and SILENCE descend as it is revealed that rather than any hostile intruder -

BRAY and TRUDY have arrived in the Mall, dumbfounded to be confronted by -

DAL but now looking like DARTH VADER, JACK in his DECONTAMINATION SUIT, also not seemingly being from this world, all the weird COSTUMES and MASKS of those in role playing dress up, along with the YOUNGSTERS in pyjamas as if they have stepped out of a surreal version of Peter Pan.

The other non-role playing RATS, all except for AMBER, have their weapons raised, at the ready.

>                    AMBER
>          Stand down. All of you.
>          These people aren't

AMBER (cont'd)
hostile.- Told you we might
expect some more company -
remember?

INT. FLAME'S INNER SANCTUM. PRIVILEGED
RESORT. NIGHT.

Flaming torches casting looming shadows.
The DISCARD girl seen in the slave fields
earlier is now rubbing the guitar she
retrieved against herself, sensuously
running her tongue across the curves of
the wood, caressing the instrument.

She is watched impassively by FLAME,
HARMONY and OX, surrounded by SERVANTS.
Some are beautiful, androgynous creatures.

One thing we can't help but notice. The
PRIVILEGED are all so good looking,
indulged, decadent, the ultimate of
what all young people suffer from peer
pressures. Don't even think about not
having the perfect body, or being super
hip, cool, attractive.

The DISCARD finally cries out in orgasmic
pleasure.

FLAME
Nice one! 54, Hohner. Pure
Ivory frets. High tension
neck action.  Sexy time!

                    HARMONY
     You want her?


                    FLAME
     H-e-l-l-o ...


As erotic as it all was - the DISCARD
doesn't do anything for FLAME and he
scoffs, almost offended.


                    FLAME
     I'm talking about the guitar
     - not 'her', Harmony! I
     mean just look at her. Can
     you imagine?


                    HARMONY
     Well, you heard the man
     himself. Lose a bit of
     weight, one day you might
     be a candidate to be
     Privileged. Right now
     you're still a Discard.
     Back to the slave fields for
     you, girl. (to Flame) Any
     reward? For retrieving the
     guitar?


                    FLAME
     Give her to Ox. A gift for
     the night. From me. Even if
     it is a bit on the big size
     - lots for you, Ox, to get
     your teeth into.

OX grins, nods to a sneering FLAME in gratitude, licks his lips. He likes the sound of that. Even if the humiliated DISCARD GIRL is clearly not as taken with the notion.

INT. SHOPPING MALL. NIGHT.

The generators are still fading, causing flickering light. JACK, DAL and their team are working on the generator nearby.

The other RATS, except the younger ones, are assembled in the food hall. And TRUDY has twinges of pain.

                    AMBER
          Sure you're ok, Trudy?

                    TRUDY
          Think so.

                    LEX
          Well, I'm sure as hell not!
          Never trusted strangers -

                    AMBER
          Told you before, Trudy
          isn't a 'stranger'. She's
          an old school friend.

                    LEX
          Wasn't just meaning her,
          Amber.

He casts a cold glance at BRAY, but is clearly threatened by his sheer presence with BRAY more than capable of taking care of himself against LEX who has always been an ace fighter, top dog.

> AMBER
> I wouldn't have retained
> Bray if I thought we
> couldn't trust him, Lex.
> Duh.

> LEX
> Duh yourself. Me and the
> Rat militia could've made
> sure Trudy got safely to
> the Mall to give birth to
> her kid if that's what you
> wanted. Didn't need to hire
> any mercenary to do that.

> AMBER
> I'm not saying you and the
> Militia aren't capable,
> Lex. But no one knows the
> sectors like Bray.

> LEX
> How do YOU know –

> AMBER
> Well, having a reputation
> like Bray sure helps. And I

AMBER (cont'd)
also thought that you might
scout a passage for us to
the Tribal gathering, Bray
- if you're available, that
is.

BRAY nods, then just listens, watching
quietly, sizing them all up as they debate
and SALENE considers AMBER in concern.

SALENE
Still think we should
attend?

AMBER
If we want to try and
negotiate a treaty.

LEX
And what's the price?

AMBER
Freedom.

LEX
'His' price.

AMBER
If you'd be happy with
fresh water again, Bray?.
We have more than enough
filtered from all the rains.

                    AMBER (cont'd)
          Thanks to Jack and Dal.

BRAY nods again. To make matters worse
for LEX, he is clocking that others are
intrigued by this enigmatic loner, with
EDEN clearly finding him attractive and
she smoulders.

                    EDEN
          Nothing else you might
          like? Or want, Bray?

                    LEX
          Oh, please. (mimics her)
          "Nothing else you might
          like? Or want?" -

JACK, DAL, and their TEAM  arrive - and
we have noticed that the lights are not
flickering.

                    JACK
          That should do it.
          Generators are all fixed up.
          Again.

                    AMBER
          Well done.

                    LEX
          Tell you what. You're always
          on about a democracy,
          Amber, so why don't we put

                    LEX (cont'd)
          it to a vote? Majority
          rules.

BRAY continues watching as LEX paces
amongst the TRIBE, TRUDY now GASPING
short breaths, trying to control more
twinges of pain.

                    LEX
          Sure I can count on
          everyone's support - or
          you're all gonna have some
          problems to contend with.

                    AMBER
          It isn't a fair vote if
          you're threatening, Lex.

                    LEX
          I'm promising. Big problems
          if we open the Mall Rats to
          a bunch of loser strays. So
          - who votes for them to go?

                    AMBER
          You can't throw them out on
          the street. Trudy's having
          a baby -

                    LEX
          Come on, who's with me?!
          We've got hardly enough

LEX (cont'd)
food as it is without more
mouths to feed.

The lights flicker once more, then darkness
descends.

JACK
Not again.

TRUDY suddenly SCREAMS - a sustained,
panicked WAIL.

AMBER
It's alright, Trudy. We'll
get the generators fixed up.

EDEN
It's not just that. I think
her waters have broken.

AMBER
Oh, God. Just try and
relax, Trudy. Everything's
going to be ok! Salene
- we need towels! Clean
blankets, Eden!

BRAY
And boiling water!

INT. ZOOT'S HEADQUARTERS. CITY CENTRE
SQUARE. NIGHT.

Flaming torches casting shadows on the
walls of the Demon Dog PRISONERS seen
earlier, now having their heads forced
down under the water in a tank.

ZOOT watches impassively nearby. The
GUARDIAN nods to the LOCO GUARDS who yank
the PRISONERS back up by the hair out of
the water. They are in an awful state,
gasping for air.

> GUARDIAN
> What were you doing? In the
> Loco sector?

> PRISONER
> Already told you. We wanted
> to try and join the Tribe.

They are dunked again.

> PRISONER
> Ok, ok! We were on a
> reconnaissance mission.

> ZOOT
> Who sent you?!

> PRISONER
> Silver Face.

> ZOOT
> Why?! What's he planning?!!

> OTHER PRISONER
> I don't know. I swear!

He is dunked again, then dragged up by the hair.

> PRISONER
> He just wanted us to check how the city is guarded.

> ZOOT
> Well, you got your answer, yeah? The city's guarded pretty damn good, I reckon!

He crosses and SCREAMS in the PRISONER'S ear.

> ZOOT
> Asked you a question, man! And I don't hear no answer!

Both PRISONERS are dunked again, then dragged to the surface.

> PRISONER
> Yeah, it's good! It's guarded good!

ZOOT
You're nothing but scum.
You know that?!

The PRISONERS nod in growing unease and
it fuels ZOOT'S disdain.

ZOOT
Look at you. Pathetic. You
should be willing to die
for your Tribe rather than
talk. But now you HAVE
talked - I'm gonna do you
both a favor, yeah? And
kill you.  After what I've
got planned, you won't want
to be around no more!

INT. BEDDING STORE. LOOTED SHOPPING MALL.
NIGHT.

With all the candles it's like the dark
ages. Grim and foreboding. Deep shadows.
Flickering light.

BRAY is wiping perspiration from TRUDY'S
forehead, tears from her eyes, while she
GASPS and GROANS.

BRAY
You're doing really well,
Trudy. Try and push again.

                    TRUDY
          I can't ... I can't ...


                    AMBER
          Yes, you can. Not long
          now. Come on, Trudy. Push.
          Harder. That's my girl.
          That's the way!

TRUDY grips, clutches at AMBER'S hand,
screams in agonizing pain.

Which penetrates and affects all the
other RATS featuring EDEN and SALENE who
watch nearby.

BRAY urging with a sense of growing
anticipation.

                    BRAY
          You're almost there. The
          baby's coming ... I can see
          it ... come on, Trudy, push
          one last time. That should
          do it.

MOUSE, SAMMY, and some of the younger
ones crawl along the floor on all fours
in the semi-darkness and hide behind
some furniture to take a wide-eyed peek,
clearly not supposed to be there.

And the sight almost makes MOUSE and
SAMMY'S stomachs turn, not quite what

they were expecting to see.

It actually makes MOUSE gag and wretch.

> MOUSE
> (undertone to Sammy)
> Oh, yuck.  That's gross!
> It's like she's being -
> tortured!

TRUDY now actually giving birth, legs apart, GROANING. BRAY and AMBER delivering the baby while the other RATS watch in awe and struggle to contain the emotion as the BABY appears.

> BRAY
> The cord! ... We've got to
> cut the cord! ....

> AMBER
> Oh, my God, Trudy - it's
> a little boy ... He's
> beautiful ...

Tears fill AMBER'S eyes, the whole event touching her so profoundly now as it even does to BRAY who cuts the cord, gives the BABY a little smack. The BABY starts to CRY along with AMBER, overcome, relieved that the BABY is safe, AMBER almost as emotionally drained and exhausted as TRUDY.

But she can't help but break into a smile
as she places the BABY in TRUDY'S arms.
TRUDY beams a smile through her own tears
too, kisses the BABY.

                    TRUDY
          Hello! Welcome to the
          world, little one.

INT. CATHEDRAL. DEMON DOG HEADQUARTERS.
DAY.

The rays of the morning sun filter through
the stained glass windows like a spiritual
awakening as we hear the familiar os sounds
of Zoot's police patrol car. SILVER FACE
addressing his fellow DEMON DOGS.

                    SILVER FACE
          Remember, be careful what
          you say. Can't trust a
          Loco. And definitely not
          Zoot. Not like him to call
          a meeting. Just never know
          where he's coming from.

Suddenly amidst a crack of shattering
glass - the CORPSE of the Demon Dog
prisoner seen earlier is now hurled
through the stained glass window -

And lays motionless amidst the shards of
glass on the floor.

SILVER FACE exchanges confused and concerned glances with the DEMON DOGS as they listen to ZOOT outside.

> ZOOT'S VOICE
> Hey, Silver Face! Why don't you and your Dogs come out here and we can talk? I've got another 'present' for you.

EXT. CATHEDRAL. SUBURBS. DAY.

SILVER FACE and the DEMON DOGS appear warily through the doors and cross down the steps towards ZOOT and the GUARDIAN protruding out of the top of ZOOT'S patrol car, Loco republican GUARDS either side.

> ZOOT
> Silver Face - how you doing, my friend?!

> SILVER FACE
> Zoot. Guardian. Good to see you.

> ZOOT
> Another beautiful day in paradise.

> SILVER FACE
> You here to trade or something? What's with our

          SILVER FACE (cont'd)
Demon Dog brother?

                    ZOOT
He was found in our sector.
Think he might have wanted
to join the Locos ... I
mean, he wouldn't have been
spying on us or anything,
would he? The Dogs and
Locos ... we've always been
friends, right?

               SILVER FACE
Always, Zoot. You know
that.

                    ZOOT
Glad to hear it. Sure the
Locos can count on your
support if Flame and the
Privileged ever fancy their
chances. So I wanted to
deliver you ... a gift.

ZOOT nods to one of his GUARDS who removes
a box from the back of the car, crosses
to the steps and hands the box to SILVER
FACE.

               SILVER FACE
          Appreciate it.

He opens the box - recoils and gags - as

he removes the bloodied, severed HEAD of the other PRISONER we saw the previous night.

                    ZOOT
          We also found him in our
          sector. Thought you might
          like to see what happens
          in the Locos if anyone
          defects. Have a nice day!
          Friend!!!

He grins coldly, nods, the police patrol car speeds off, the GUARDS roller blading either side. SILVER FACE and the DEMON DOGS gaze in horror at the severed head.

EXT. RESORT. BEACH.  DAY.

The base of the PRIVILEGED, a once luxurious but now decaying tropical resort. Thatched beach huts, sun beds round a salt water pool.

Some of the PRIVILEGED are surfing, others swimming, others lifting weights, some even just tanning their already brown, beautiful bodies while being fed fresh fruit from the ANDROGYNOUS SERVANTS.

A vision of paradise. But this isn't beach/surfing culture, or a look from any travel magazines.

No swimsuits. More loin clothes. The

aesthetic, fashion, make up, VERY Tribal. Faces streaked by paint, coconut and sea shell jewelry, bone earrings, feathers intertwined with palm leaf beaded hair extensions.

War canoes are being hand carved, icons, faces of Flame, almost as a god, at the bow are being painted.

Some of the GIRLS are topless while weaving flaxen from plants.

Others getting tattoos, body piercing with striking designs.

And we can see why these young people are members of the PRIVILEGED. They look so fit, tanned, extraordinarily lithe, sensual, VERY attractive. For all that it is somehow almost primitive, part from the past, it is also part never really quite seen before. As if from the future.

Suddenly we hear panicked - YELLING.

INT. HALLWAY. PRIVILEGED RESORT. DAY.

HARMONY walks briskly down the hallway, half running, responding.

> FLAME OS.
> Harmony! Help! Quick! Help
> me! No! NOOOOOOOO!!!!!

She arrives at a door, outside of which OX is standing guard.

> HARMONY
> What's the problem?!

> OX
> Dunno. The master just started freaking out. Won't let me in.

INT. FLAME'S INNER SANCTUM. PRIVILEGED RESORT. DAY.

ECU reflection in a hand held mirror of a panicked wild EYE. Finally revealing HARMONY bursting in.

> HARMONY
> What's going on, what's wrong?!

> FLAME
> This!!!

He indicates a spot on his face, then hurls the mirror across the room. Thrusts one hand across his cheek to hide the spot. Kicks furniture, throws guitars against the wall to punctuate each of his words of anguish, utter distress. In the mother of all temper tantrums. Total meltdown.

FLAME

Where did it come from?!
That slave girl bitch?!
Think I caught it from
her?!

HARMONY

Try and calm down, Flame.
Could just be down to
something you've eaten.

But it just fuels the anger. He is in
absolute torment, wrath.

FLAME

I AM Privileged! I don't do
spots! I'm not some oily
skinned Discard! Someone
impure! I am perfect! And I
want whoever is responsible
to be found?!!!

HARMONY

How do you figure I can do
that?

FLAME

That's your problem,
Harmony. I want whoever it
is to be punished, OK?  No,
tortured! Yeah, tortured
till they wail like a
Fender Telecaster!!! I mean
it!!!

HARMONY watches him kick over another chair, then suddenly clearly has a strategy.

>                    HARMONY
>           Come to think of it, maybe
>           it was the slave girl. Did
>           you check out that skin? I
>           did. Yuck. Gross!

>                    FLAME
>           Exactly.

>                    HARMONY
>           If that Discard chick
>           looked up the meaning of
>           ugly in a dictionary -
>           she'd see a photo of her
>           ugly mug there.

>                    FLAME
>           Bitch!

>                    HARMONY
>           I'll deal with her, I
>           promise ... long as you do
>           something for me? You need
>           to check out the Militia,
>           put in an appearance, let
>           them know you think the
>           training is going well.

FLAME is calming now but sighs, almost a

whine, like a child.

                    FLAME
          Do I have to?


                  HARMONY
          Small price to pay to rule
          the world, Flame.

But FLAME is preoccupied, gazing in the
mirror again, more interested in the spot
and he pinches two fingers together to try
and pop it.

INT. LOOTED SHOPPING MALL. DAY.

BRAY arrives in the bedding section of
a department store, crosses to TRUDY,
their delivery in undertones so as not
to waken the BABY who is in a crib by the
side of TRUDY'S bed.


                    BRAY
          How are you doing? You ok?
          (she nods) What about the
          baby?


                   TRUDY
          I've been thinking the
          same thing. Is it right.
          Bringing a baby into this
          world. I mean what kind of
          future does he have -

> BRAY
> He IS the future, Trudy.
> That's all that matters. So
> never question if you did
> the right thing.

> TRUDY
> What about you, Bray ...
> you're not going to leave,
> are you?

> BRAY
> Just because I do - doesn't
> mean to say you have to as
> well, Trudy.

> TRUDY
> Don't know if I could ever
> settle here. Even if that
> creepy Lex wanted me to.

> BRAY
> You don't have to make any
> decision now.

> TRUDY
> Nor you. Please stay, Bray.
> Even for a little while. Me
> and the baby, we need you.

IN THE FOOD HALL

Some of the older RATS, featuring LEX

playing on a pinball machine nearby, are watching MOUSE and SAMMY, intrigued and sympathetic while they prepare food, eat.

The younger RATS are suffering their first day of school, AMBER writing numbers on a flip chart.

> AMBER
> And it's just so important to try and understand the structure of all these numbers ... It's called tables.

> MOUSE
> What's the difference between THOSE tables? And THESE tables?

> AMBER
> There's a big difference, Mouse -

> MOUSE
> Then how come they have the same name?

> AMBER
> I don't know. They just do.

LEX

It was just like that in the
old world, Mouse. Before
the darkness. Teachers
always thought they knew it
all. But when it came right
down to it - they knew
nothing. Diddley squat.

AMBER

Don't start, Lex. Not now.
Please!

LEX

Yeah, well, I just don't
think we should look at
the old ways. Teachers and
schools suck. There are no
rules. Not any more. We can
all be whatever we want to
be.

EDEN

Interesting. Given that
people see things not as
they ARE. More as the way
THEY are.

LEX

Ohhhhhh! Earth to Eden.
What the hell does that
mean?

                    AMBER
        Maybe if you had paid a
        little more attention at
        school, Lex, you might have
        found the answer.

He scoffs as AMBER writes the tables on
the chart.

                    AMBER
        You and everyone might
        be sitting at one kind
        of table, Mouse ... but
        these are different kinds
        of tables. And you need
        to learn them to get an
        understanding of basic
        arithmetic.

                    LEX
        And then you can count all
        your money. Which you don't
        even know what it is. At
        all the banks which aren't
        here anymore -

                    AMBER
        You are such a pain at
        times, Lex! I've just about
        had enough! I mean it!

                    LEX
        Just saying ...

AMBER

You might find this hard to believe - but there ARE other things in addition to 'fists' which give people power.

LEX

Oh, really. Like?

AMBER

Knowledge! The need for education. Unless of course you think that's all down to learning how to arm wrestle.

LEX

Don't knock it! Or next time the Locos or any other Tribe attacks - don't call me if they don't run like hell with all the Mall Rat warriors going over their scary 10 times tables! Cause it ain't gonna help!

EDEN

Amber's right, Lex. We all need to learn to be as strong and healthy as we can. Not only in our bodies. But in our spirit,

> EDEN (cont'd)
> the soul - AND the mind.

> LEX
> And then just hope we all
> don't drop dead from the
> virus. Or whatever the hell
> it was that wiped all the
> adults and everyone out -

> AMBER
> Lex! ENOUGH!!!

> LEX
> I just don't get it. What
> good's it all going to do?

> AMBER
> A lot of good. And you're
> not going to wear me down
> on this. So it's a waste of
> time to keep trying!

LEX scoffs, sneers and continues with the
pin ball game.

AMBER glares angrily at him, then sighs
to compose herself before addressing the
class. MOUSE gives her a huge fake smile.
And AMBER returns it.

> AMBER
> Let's go through it again
> ...

EXT. RESORT. BEACH.  DAY.

The PRIVILEGED Tribe notice FLAME and
HARMONY nearby, surrounded by OX and his
team of SECURITY. All gaze awestruck,
some even bow in deference, while others
excitedly converge.

                    HARMONY
          Don't try to touch. Even
          look.

Those of the PRIVILEGED converging humbly
avert their gaze.

FLAME is taking no chances though. He has
one hand slightly covering his cheek and
fakes a smile to all as the DELEGATION
cross to and walk up steps onto -

A DAIS

overlooking a clearing where the MILITIA
are training.

They look VERY threatening, intimidating,
their faces tattooed.

Some are doing hand to hand combat
with the skills of the best in martial
art, others are stepping through tires,
crawling under roped tunnels.

When they notice FLAME, HARMONY and
the SECURITY, they immediately marshal

together, looking very fierce as they step
and CHANT, like a haka to honor him.

FLAME waves, acknowledging them, but it's
all phoney as he is clearly not into it
and his delivery is in an undertone to
HARMONY.

> FLAME
> Right, that's me done.
> Let's split. Get out of
> here.

> HARMONY
> Not yet. You need to say a
> few words.

> FLAME
> Like what?

HARMONY feeds discreet lines in an
undertone and FLAME repeats them while
addressing the MILITIA.

> HARMONY/FLAME
> Brothers and Sisters of
> The Privileged. The Tribal
> Gathering approaches.
> Leaders have no hope of
> extending any kind of
> treaty. So all warriors
> have to be prepared for
> battle. Where they will be
> expected to make the

> HARMONY/FLAME (cont'd)
> ultimate sacrifice in the
> event of war!

The MILITIA erupts in a frenzied CHANTING in unison.

> MILITIA
> Bring it!  Flame!!! Flame!!!
> FLAME!!!

INT. LOOTED SHOPPING MALL. DAY.

AMBER indicates the numbers on the flip chart.

> AMBER
> Now, Sammy - lets go
> through it one more time.
> One times one is ....?

> SAMMY
> One.

> AMBER
> Right. Good. And two times
> two is .... Mouse?

> MOUSE
> .... twenty-two?

> AMBER
> No. It's four.

>                    MOUSE
>      Why?

>                    AMBER
>      Try and stick with me on
>      this, Mouse, and I'll try
>      and explain. Again.

She passes some apples and oranges to the
class.

>                    AMBER
>      Two apples. Two oranges.
>      Let's count them up and see
>      how many pieces of fruit
>      you all have. One, two,
>      three - four, right?

>                    MOUSE
>      Wrong!

>                    AMBER
>      It's four, Mouse.

>                    MOUSE
>      No - it's three.

>                    AMBER
>      No, four, Mouse. Look -
>      one, two, three, four -

>                    MOUSE
>      Not for Sammy it isn't!

SAMMY is biting into one of the apples and AMBER sighs in growing frustration.

The sudden sound of the baby CRYING os.

>                    MOUSE
>      Can I go and play with the
>      baby?

>                    AMBER
>      The baby isn't a doll,Mouse.
>      And school just can't end
>      just when you feel like
>      it - especially when we've
>      hardly even started.

>                    EDEN
>      Might not be a bad idea,
>      Amber. Difficult enough for
>      them all to concentrate.

>                    AMBER
>      Tell me about it. Ok -
>      Class dismissed. We'll come
>      back to it another day.

The YOUNGER RATS eagerly disperse to fix something for them to eat.

AMBER sure looks as if she is more the one in need of a break as she crosses to a counter, pours herself a drink where DAL and JACK are filling tanks.

                    AMBER
I'm starting to go off this
idea. In a big way.


                    JACK
Maybe some of the younger
ones might be better off
helping me and Dal. Learn
to do something practical -


                    AMBER
Such as?


                    JACK
They could collect up stuff
for the Gathering for a
start -


                    AMBER
Why? So YOU can be let off
duties? And have more time
to come up with some new
role playing games?


                    JACK
                (it did)
Never crossed our mind,
right, Dal?


                    DAL
Oh, right. Absolutely,
Amber.

LEX still playing the pin ball machine reacts to the os sounds of the baby crying.

>           LEX
>      That kid wailing - it's
>      driving me nuts!

>           SALENE
>      Not the poor baby's fault,
>      Lex.

He crosses to her, kisses the back of her neck.

>           LEX
>      If you're such a big fan of
>      it - how about you and me
>      put on a display and give
>      these younger ones some
>      REAL lessons? On how to
>      make babies, eh?

>           MOUSE
>      Yeah, that's a great idea,
>      Lex. We need more babies.

MOUSE is now sitting eating at a table with SAMMY and watches a bit confused as SALENE pushes him away.

>           SALENE
>      You really are disgusting
>      at times, you know that?

                    LEX
        Couldn't seem to get enough
        of it the other night.


                   EDEN
        You both ... together?


                  SALENE
        Not for long if he keeps on
        like this.


                    LEX
        No need to be jealous,
        Eden. More than enough of
        Lexy sexy boy to go around.


                   EDEN
        In your dreams!


                  AMBER
        Come on, Lex. Try and be
        careful what you say in
        front of the little ones,
        will you?

LEX crosses to AMBER.


                    LEX
        What? The teacher doesn't
        want them to learn about
        sex?

> AMBER
> They've just started their
> times tables, give them a
> chance.

> LEX
> How about when they're ready
> - you and I teach them?
> Always wondered what you'd
> be like in bed. Underneath
> all that goody two shoes -
> bet you'd be wicked -

He reaches out to stroke her hair, but
she hurls her bottle of water into his
face and elbows him in the gut.

> AMBER
> That's one thing you'll
> never ever find out, Lex. So
> I suggest you occupy that
> pea brain of yours with
> some other thoughts.

BRAY arrives.

> BRAY
> Trudy was hoping she could
> get something to eat.

> AMBER
> Sure. Can you organize
> something, Salene?

SALENE nods, moves into the kitchen area
while LEX crosses to BRAY.

                    LEX
          Don't know if I made myself
          clear the other night. But
          what food we have ... it's
          for the Mall Rats.


                    AMBER
          Trudy can have some of
          my share. And you, Bray.
          Really, we have more than
          enough to go around.


                    BRAY
          Sure?


                    EDEN
          Absolutely. Don't pay any
          attention to Lex.

LEX squares menacingly up to BRAY.

                    LEX
          If you don't - I might have
          to look for other 'ways'
          for you to understand.


                    BRAY
          Oh, really?

Raymond Thompson

                    LEX
          Yeah, really! So you and
          that lady friend of yours
          and her kid might be doing
          yourselves a big favour if
          you decide to move on. If
          you get my drift!

BRAY outstretches one arm, clenches a
fist, inches from LEX'S face and there
is an ominous power in his quiet self
control, harnessing all his contained
pent up aggression.

                    BRAY
          Give it up, Lex! Ever since
          I've arrived - I've been
          watching you. And I've got
          you all figured out! I'm
          bigger than you. Stronger
          than you. Braver than you.
          Wiser than you. And I don't
          want to hear another word
          about when we might leave.
          I can't speak for Trudy.
          But I'll be heading off
          when I'm good and ready.
          Not when you are. 'If you
          get MY drift'!

                    AMBER
          Is there ... ah, ...
          anything else you want to
          go over with Bray, Lex?

                    LEX
          Oh, yeah! But I'll save
          it right now. For another
          time.

He glares threateningly at BRAY who glares
back for a beat. Then BRAY withdraws his
outstretched arm as LEX turns, leaves.

                    AMBER
          Might be a little hard to
          believe ... but when you
          get to know Lex ... under
          all those defences he puts
          up -  he's really quite a
          nice guy.

                    BRAY
          Yeah, seems like it.

                    AMBER
          And no matter what he says
          - after the gathering, you
          and Trudy and the baby are
          welcome to stay as long as
          you like.

                    BRAY
          Thanks. Appreciate it. I'll
          go and give Salene a hand.

BRAY crosses into the food hall towards
SALENE. EDEN and AMBER watching him go.

                    EDEN
Did you feel the force of
that?


                    AMBER
Lex certainly did. And it
serves him right.


                    EDEN
Are Bray and Trudy an item?


                    AMBER
Don't think so. Why?
Interested?


                    EDEN
The wind can be so gentle.
And yet also so strong. But
no-one will ever be able to
predict it, control it, own
it, let alone ... touch it.


                    AMBER
Well, I can always rely on
you for an interesting way
of 'looking' at things,
Eden.


                    EDEN
Are you, Amber, interested?


                    AMBER
Bray's a gun for hire. And

                    AMBER (cont'd)
          his skills will be useful.
          Nothing less. Nothing more.

She sounds more convinced than she looks
which registers with EDEN.

EXT. CITY. DESERTED STREETS. NIGHT.

Loco GUARDS step to one side as a rider
gallops though a barricade, reigns his
mount, leaps off and crosses briskly to
the city hall headquarters.

INT. ZOOT'S HEADQUARTERS. CITY HALL.
NIGHT.

ZOOT working out, unleashing powerful
blows into a punch bag with a manic,
angry intensity.

The GUARDIAN enters.

                    GUARDIAN
          News. From an informant. The
          militia of the Privileged
          are being trained, preparing
          for .... something.

                    ZOOT
          Only one thing they need
          to prepare for is - being
          under the Locos' rule!

                    GUARDIAN
Think they might have a
different take on it, Zoot.
We've got to be careful
they don't try and invade.


                      ZOOT
Why don't we just 'take'
the fight to them?


                    GUARDIAN
We don't know what kind of
support they have. From the
other Tribes.


                      ZOOT
Neither do they. The Locos
could put together an
awesome invasion force of
our own, Guardian.


                    GUARDIAN
You're leader, Zoot. And can
call it as you see it. I'm
just an advisor. And that
would be ... we need the
numbers. From all I hear -
the Privileged militia seem
to be impressive.


                      ZOOT
These informants ... are
they reliable?

                    GUARDIAN
          They know what to expect
          if not. So - what do you
          reckon?


                    ZOOT
          We attend this Gathering.
          See what all the leaders
          have to say. Who's with us.
          Who's against us. But one
          thing's for sure. If The
          Privileged want to mix it
          with us - it's on!


EXT. CAR DEALERSHIP. SUBURBIA. DAY.

SALENE watches LEX hurling a brick,
shattering a mammoth pane of glass,
outside a once upmarket but now decayed
car dealership, giving vent to his pent
up anger.


                    SALENE
          Well? .... Feel better?


                    LEX
          No! I'm telling you, that
          Bray ... he's got it
          coming.


                    SALENE
          I don't know about that,
          Lex. He seems like he can
          take care of himself.

                    LEX
          So can I.


                   SALENE
          It's not a competition.

INT. CAR DEALERSHIP. DAY.

LEX and SALENE enter, gaze around,
despondently.

                   SALENE
          Doesn't seem to be much of
          anything of any value to
          trade here.

                    LEX
          No ....

Only some of the most expensive cars ever
seen in our world. Including a Ferrari.
And LEX gazes longingly at it.

                    LEX
          Look at that, babe. Hard
          to believe that would have
          been of value once. In the
          old world.

He crosses to the car and runs his hand
lovingly over the body while SALENE
searches drawers, files, desks.

                    LEX
        If anyone was lucky enough
        to take this beauty for a
        spin - bet it'd have been
        like riding a thousand wild
        horses. Or even you.


                  SALENE
        That supposed to be a
        compliment?

She gathers up some fading leather
binders while LEX is totally preoccupied,
unscrewing the gas tank cap of the Ferrari.


                  SALENE
        These might be worth
        something. To someone.
        Never know.

LEX sniffs at the opening to the gas
tank, registers sudden hope, then pushes
the body of the car in growing urgency,
listening for any swirling liquid.


                  SALENE
        What are you doing?!


                    LEX
        About to check out if I
        still remember how to hot
        wire, Sal. Think we're in
        luck!

EXT. PERIMETERS. LOOTED SHOPPING MALL. DAY.

DAL and JACK, MOUSE, SAMMY, along with some of our n/s regular RATS we have seen before, are digging up potatoes and other vegetables in a patch of waste ground, the mall visible in the near distance.

A sudden crack of engine noise, skidding. DAL, JACK, the RATS turn.

And gaze at the Ferrari, appearing around a corner, fishtailing as it roars past in a speeding blur and recedes down a street.

INT. FERRARI. TRAVELLING. DAY.

SALENE, in the passenger seat clings uneasily as LEX goes through the gears, accelerating.

The rev and speedometer dials increasing as the vehicle quickly increases even more in speed.

> LEX
> Just feel the power. Oh,
> man, this thing rocks!

EXT. SUBURBS. DAY.

The Ferrari roaring through the deserted streets, towards  an entrance ramp – and onto the freeway.

EXT. FREEWAY. DAY.

The Ferrari hurling along the abandoned, ghostly freeway ... faster ... faster.

INT. FERRARI. TRAVELLING. DAY.

From the dials we can see that LEX is really pushing it now to almost maximum speed.

And although SALENE swallows nervously at the passing blur out of the windows she is as exhilarated as LEX.

Suddenly the engine dies and the car slows.

> LEX
> Damn! Must be out of gas.

EXT. FREEWAY. DAY.

The Ferrari draws to a stop. The doors open, LEX and SALENE get out.

> SALENE
> So what do we do now? Call a taxi?

> LEX
> Shut it!

                    SALENE
          Well, I'd say it looks like
          we're in for a bit of a
          walk. Just hope we're not
          THAT far out of the Mall
          Rat sector.

She gazes around in growing unease as
they start on the walk.

And we crane back to a high angle to
fully portray our urban landscape of the
once heavily populated but now mostly
uninhabited suburbs and the ghostly city
visible in the distance.

Most of all though, a high angle to
punctuate the solitary image of LEX and
SALENE walking along the deserted freeway
from the abandoned Ferrari, both doors
left wide open.

INT. SHOPPING MALL. DAY.

EDEN unlocks a freezer, removes leaves
and plants, turns.

And is almost run over by SAMMY in a
wire shopping trolley, which speeds
past, MOUSE suspended, riding on the hand
railing rather than pushing it.

                    EDEN
          Careful! Or someone could
          end up getting hurt.- Like

                    EDEN (cont'd)
    me.

The trolley smashes into an aisle. And we
can see now that we are in a supermarket,
but the aisles are bare of any product or
produce. Those days have long gone.

                    EDEN
        Give me a hand with this,
        will you, please?

MOUSE pushes SAMMY in the trolley to EDEN.
Then helps gather and pass the leaves and
plants, along with cases of herbs and
spices to SAMMY who stacks it all neatly
in the cart.

                    MOUSE
        What IS all this stuff?

                    EDEN
        Medicine. For us to trade.
        Least it will be when I
        grind it all up and bottle
        it.

                    MOUSE
        Doesn't look like it'd be
        worth much.

                    EDEN
        Never just rely on your
        eyes, Mouse. Or you, Sammy.

                    EDEN (cont'd)
          Your eyes can deceive you.
          You have to look deeper.

She twists some leaves, passes them to
SAMMY and MOUSE to hold.

                         EDEN
          What do you think these
          are?

                        SAMMY
          Leaves.

                         EDEN
          Not just any kind of leaves.
          They are - dock leaves. If
          you ever see any nettles
          you'll always find these
          growing. Right nearby. And
          if you ever got stung ...
          say - there -

She rubs a leaf on her hand to demonstrate.

                         EDEN
          You rub the dock leaf where
          the nettle sting is and
          - what do you think will
          happen?

                        MOUSE
          You have to go and wash a
          smelly, messy hand.

EDEN

No ...

SAMMY

You get stung again?

EDEN

The natural world never
works that way, Sammy. The
dock leaf would stop all
the pain from the stinging.
Completely. Isn't that
amazing?

She continues to load the cart.

EDEN

All natural herbal remedies
and cures are always
best. And all you have
to do is look to all the
plants which grow, get in
tune with them, try to
understand them - and thank
our Mother Earth for such
precious gifts.

MOUSE

Didn't work out that way
for all the adults though.

EDEN deadpans. She considers MOUSE, who
innocently wasn't trying to make a point
- though she has, a profound point to

EDEN. She sadly sighs, reflects.

> EDEN
> No. Unfortunately not
> all people were tuned
> in, Mouse. Otherwise we
> wouldn't have been left in
> - and inherited - such a
> mess.

IN THE MAIN SQUARE.

A hive of activity. TRUDY with the BABY
strapped in a cloth papoose is standing
with some RATS behind long tables, boxing
up produce and an assortment of items to
be traded.

And we find AMBER and SALENE carrying boxes
and stacking them in carts and trolleys
nearby.

> AMBER
> Just a few more. Then we're
> done.

> SALENE
> Hope so - I'm exhausted.

> AMBER
> I'm not surprised. You've
> got to be careful, Salene.
> Not just taking a walk
> through unknown sectors.

                    AMBER (cont'd)
          But with Lex? He's like a
          missile. Point him in the
          right direction and he has
          a chance of getting a good
          result. But if he strays
          off target ...


                    SALENE
          Yeah, I know. I've always
          seemed to go for the type
          that I think I can 'tame'.
          Never seems to work out
          that way.


DAL and JACK wheeling barrows laden with
produce we saw them harvest earlier past
LEX - and he calls them over.


                    LEX
          Hey, guys.


He is sitting bathing his sore feet in a
bowl of water after his walk. LEX gazes
around, his delivery in an undertone with
more than a hint of conspiracy as DAL and
JACK arrive.


                    LEX
          After you finish with that,
          don't forget the 'water'.


                    JACK
          You've already got water.

                    LEX
For somebody heading our
intelligence unit - you've
never struck me as being
too smart, you know that?
I'm not talking about water
for my feet. I'm talking
about THE water ... water
...


                    JACK
Oh, I get it. THE water.
Water.


BRAY is loading boxes onto a trolley as
AMBER arrives.


                    AMBER
How is it all going, Bray?
Got all you need? For the
tolls?


                    BRAY
Yeah, I'm pretty much
there. Though I might need
something a little extra
special. As a gift for
Hawk.


                    AMBER
I'm not so sure we should
go through the Eco sector,
Bray.

                    BRAY
          It'll save about twenty
          hours.


                    AMBER
          But even so ... the Ecos?


                    BRAY
          I've scouted all round that
          area many times. And never
          had any problems, Amber.
          You don't want to cross
          Hawk and the Ecos. Ever.
          But they're fair people ...
          just as long as we are.


AMBER considers him, then nods.


                    AMBER
          Ok. If you're sure.


EXT. FOREST. DAY.


A hand covered with bangles of bones
carefully draws back a branch.


And we see through the foliage a line of
RATS approaching along a track.


BRAY is leading the long line through the
dense forest. The RATS are travelling with
all they have to trade at the Gathering
conveyed in baby carriages, trolleys,
back packs, wheel barrows, push bikes,

towing carts.

And all are a little uneasy as the morning mist hangs eerily all around.

SUBJECTIVE CAMERA

Through the trees and undergrowth watching the RATS and moving in ominously ... closer ... closer ... as if they are prey.

BRAY suddenly stops, indicates for all the RATS to do the same.

He listens to the sounds of the birds seemingly calling to each other. And like the experienced scout that he is - BRAY knows. And he speaks quietly, calmly.

> BRAY
> Everybody ... don't say a word ... I want you to stay still ... just don't react to anything ... anything at all.

The RATS don't move, frozen in tense anticipation - but steal cautious glances out of the corners of their eyes.

Nothing.

The RATS stand rigid in the uneasy silence, broken only by an occasional bird cry.

After a long beat.

                    LEX
          This is crazy! Come on.
          Let's make a move. We can't
          just stand waiting here
          forever, let's ....

BRAY glares at LEX whose words have
trailed off as the forest suddenly seems
to come alive.

Alive with ECOS appearing from everywhere,
all over the dense forest - and it almost
takes the RATS' breath away.

Especially LEX, who is gazing down the
end of a long spear.

The ECOS seem to be all around, some even
perched high up in the trees - it is an
overwhelming, awesome sight.

All raising weapons, spears, long bows,
and looking to be only part human but part
plant, like living tree people, their
bodies covered with branches, leaves,
necklaces of bark, bones.

But it is their faces that are so fierce
and striking.

Caked by mud and painted all white, with
streaks of red - like blood - around the
eyes, their hair a deep forest green,

extended by intertwined plaited stripped flaxen and plants.

For all that it is primitive, native, it is also as if these people are from a totally different planet.

Particularly the leader, HAWK, who appears through the trees. He is wearing a magnificent headdress of colored feathers and for all his threatening look exudes dignity. Power.

MOUSE and SAMMY cling to AMBER and EDEN as HAWK crosses to BRAY, nods.

> HAWK
>
> Bray ....

> BRAY
>
> How are you, Hawk? It's
> been a while.

They exchange a clenched fist greeting, then HAWK indicates and the ECOS lower their weapons.

> BRAY
>
> This is the Mall Rats.
> They're attending a
> Gathering. In sector seven.
> And they'd like to offer
> a toll. For safe passage
> through the forest ....

                    BRAY (cont'd)
             Your forest ....


                      HAWK
             We need no toll from a
             friend, Bray.

DAL and JACK exchange an uneasy glance,
their delivery in an undertone.

                      DAL
             With friends like that ...
             you'd have NO enemies.


                      JACK
             Or even end up on a menu.
             Dead.  These people. Man.
             Freaky.


                      BRAY
             Please accept it all as a
             gift then, Hawk. It would
             be an honor for you to take
             it.

AMBER pushes a cart forward laden with
fruit and vegetables and BRAY hands HAWK
a pendant. He accepts it graciously, with
great dignity and nods.


                      HAWK
             The honour is to know you.
             And to have the respect you
             show for the ways of our

                HAWK (cont'd)
        people. You're always
        welcome here, Bray. Travel
        safely, friend.


EXT. TRIBAL GATHERING MONTAGE. DAY.

GUARDS from different TRIBES are checking for weapons to be left at the 'gate' at the barricaded entrance.

Beyond we take in the full flavor and color, a real visual spectacle. Tents, trade, fresh produce on stalls, sheep and cattle being herded amongst the CROWDS. Music, break-dance competitions. A gathering of the TRIBES, an array of wild make up, grungy fashion, young people expressing themselves extolling a variety of various looks, cultures of all attending.

Feathers, war paint, avant garde, elemental, futuristic. Some have even adapted welding masks and have hair extensions of twisted wire and feathers, everything and anything scavenged from the breakdown of society to make a fashion or identity statement.

SALENE AND TRUDY

With the BABY on TRUDY'S back, tied in a sheet like a papoose strapped diagonally around her shoulders, are at a stall examining clothes for trade.

FEATURING BRAY

Watching EDEN in the dancing competition - and she sure can dance.

But there is an introspective moment as EDEN glances across the CROWD, as if her graceful, sensual movements are designed just for BRAY. Which indeed they are.

And BRAY knows it.

LEX, DAL AND JACK

Are at a stall, unscrupulously trading a supposed antidote to the virus, LEX handing a small bottle of water to a CUSTOMER.

> LEX
> There you go, partner. I wish you a long and happy life.

JACK, uneasy, steers LEX for a quite word.

> JACK
> Lex ... I don't like this.

> LEX
> I do.

> DAL
> I don't feel right about it

                    DAL (cont'd)
          either, Lex.


                    LEX
          We're raking it in. Look -
          booze, blankets, batteries.
          If we get lucky, maybe even
          sex.


                    JACK
                (a bit tempted now)
          You ... think?


                    LEX
          All kinds of stuff. So shut
          it and let's get on with
          it.


                    DAL
          Yeah, but what happens if
          we also get caught?!

INT. TENT. TRIBAL GATHERING. DAY.

AMBER trying to obtain the support to
extend the treaty from the LEADERS and
ADVISORS of the Tribes.

                    AMBER
          The treaty has worked so
          well for so long now. I
          know we've all had our
          differences -

                    HARMONY
Is that what you call it?


                    AMBER
Ok, disagreements. But the
Mall Rats just think it
would make sense to commit
to all the principles
again. Recognizing the
right of each Tribe to
live at peace. In their own
sectors - with no fear of
anyone trying to invade. Or
to make any kind of claim.


                    ZOOT
Who said anything about ...
invading?


                    AMBER
You can't deny there's been
talk, Zoot. And that won't
achieve anything. If we
could just form alliances.
That would be better than
having warring Tribes. Then
maybe we could all think
of introducing a social
charter. For law and order
... peoples' rights  ...


There  is  an  underlying  tension,  an
atmosphere  of  mistrust  -  and  something
chilling  about  the  deeply  intense  way

FLAME is staring transfixed at ZOOT while
HARMONY tries to broker a deal.

> HARMONY
> The Privileged MIGHT agree
> ... if we take over sector
> 5 ...

> AMBER
> Think you're missing my
> point, Harmony.

> HARMONY
> You mean the Locos. They've
> been after taking control
> of sector 5. From the Demon
> Dogs, from what we hear.

> SILVER FACE
> And if we gave you control
> of sector 5 - what would we
> get?

> HARMONY
> Crops ... grain ... sure we
> could work something out.

> ZOOT
> Don't think the Dogs would
> be interested, right?

He casts SILVER FACE a threatening look
and he shakes his head - no.

                    AMBER
What do you have to say
about it, Flame?


                    HARMONY
He's cool.


                    AMBER
Why don't you let Flame
speak for himself?


                    HARMONY
He does.


                    AMBER
No, you just did, Harmony.
I asked Flame - remember?


                    HARMONY
                    (Ice)
I said he was cool with it!


                    AMBER
                    (Ice)
But HE didn't!


                    ZOOT
What's with him anyway?!
What the hell is he staring
at?! Is he stoned? On kava,
or something?!


                    131

Still FLAME just stares at ZOOT. Intensely. Not even a blink.

> HARMONY
> Flame relies on me for advice, that's all. And if I'm cool, then Flame's cool.

> ZOOT
> You better 'advise' him to stop checking me out. It's starting to freak me, man! Big time!!!

But FLAME continues staring intently, blankly at ZOOT while AMBER diplomatically tries to diffuse matters.

> AMBER
> Look, why don't we get back to discussing the treaty and a bill of rights? Try and get it signed off. For everyone's sake. It really is the only way to secure the future. For ALL the Tribes.

EXT. TRIBAL GATHERING. DAY.

In the dancing area the MALL RATS, featuring TRUDY, SALENE, BRAY and EDEN, wait in eager anticipation as the DJ announces.

>                    DJ
>      We got the results of the
>      break dance competition
>      now. In third place, Angel
>      Infusion of the Roosters.
>      Second place, Moon-glow
>      from Golden Dawn. And in
>      first place ... give it up -
>      for Eden of the Mall Rats!

The CROWD CHEER and BRAY, SALENE and
TRUDY WHOOP it up.

EDEN crosses to the stage on which a dune
buggy is on display and is presented with
a set of keys and a Trophy.

>                    DJ
>      There you go!
>      Congratulations.

EDEN nods in gratitude, waves,
acknowledging the CROWD as she crosses
with the keys and trophy to BRAY, TRUDY
and SALENE.

>                   BRAY
>      Well done!

>                  SALENE
>      That's awesome, Eden!

                    TRUDY
Wish I could dance like
that.


                    EDEN
More down to the Spirit
of my  animal, the Snow
Leopard. I was in tune.


                    BRAY
So what are you going to do
with the dune buggy?


                    EDEN
Try and trade something for
a few litres of gas. Think
the Locos seem to control
most of what's left these
days. If I have any luck -
I'll take you all for a joy
ride.


                    TRUDY
Don't think you'd be that
interested would you,
Salene? Not after that walk
you had a while back with
Lex.


SALENE  smiles  despite  herself  at  the
thought.

                    EDEN
      And I don't think you and
      the baby would be up for it
      either, Trudy. So it seems
      as if that just leaves you,
      Bray.

TRUDY and SALENE exchange a sick glance
at the soupçon of flirtation as EDEN looks
over her shoulder and casts a seductive
smile at BRAY while she slinks away.

AT A STALL

SAMMY watches MOUSE throw a dagger
with all her might at a target in the
distance. But the dagger embeds way off
the centre of the target and MOUSE GROANS
in frustration.

                    MOUSE
      Ah! I almost got it!

                 STALL HOLDER
      Want another go?

                    MOUSE
      I've got nothing left to
      trade. So why don't you
      just give the chicken to
      me? P-L-E-A-S-E?!

She looks such an angel but the STALL
HOLDER won't melt.

                    STALL HOLDER
          Sorry. No can do.


                    MOUSE
          Is it true it lays poisoned
          eggs that kill you?


                    STALL HOLDER
          What?!


                    MOUSE
          That's what we heard.
          Didn't we, Sammy?

SAMMY is confused - huh? And she gives
him a kick.

                    SAMMY
          Oh, yeah. Right.


                    MOUSE
          Poisoned eggs. That make
          you die. A long, painful
          death! I'm talking real
          agony ...


                    STALL HOLDER
          Nice try, little one. But I
          wasn't born yesterday.

He moves off to serve another CUSTOMER
as BRAY arrives, slightly amused, yet
sympathetic to see MOUSE so frustrated

and despondent.

                    BRAY
        What's up?


                    MOUSE
        I've been trying to win
        that chicken! I LOVE it.
        It's so cute. But it's not
        fair. No-one could EVER
        be expected to hit that
        target. Impossible!


                    BRAY
        What's the deal?


                    STALL HOLDER
        Well, like she said ... hit
        the target and you walk
        away with the chicken. Miss
        it and I keep whatever you
        got to trade. You want a
        go?


                    BRAY
        I ... don't have much. Just
        a few sticks of gum.


                    STALL HOLDER
        You got it.  One try.


BRAY exchanges the sticks of gum for the
dagger.

He eyes the dagger, breathes deeply, eyes the target as if charting the dagger's course then spins, throws.

And hits the target. Easily.

MOUSE, SAMMY and a gathering CROWD are impressed, cheer.

>                    MOUSE
>      Awesome. How'd you know how
>      to do that?!

>                    BRAY
>      Ah, just luck, I reckon.

The STALL HOLDER isn't as thrilled as MOUSE as he hands over the squawking chicken.

>                    STALL HOLDER
>      Luck?! Man, you must have
>      been practising for a
>      thousand years. There you
>      go. Careful with those
>      eggs, eh?

MOUSE fakes a smile to the STALL HOLDER and we go with her, SAMMY and BRAY. MOUSE clutches the chicken under one arm, then holds BRAY'S hand with her other spare arm.

                    BRAY
      Eggs?


                    MOUSE
      He's just jealous. Of MY
      chicken! Said it lays
      poisoned eggs. But he was
      just tricking. Right,
      Sammy? So no-one else would
      want it.


                    SAMMY
      Right.


                    MOUSE
      But I do. And I'm going to
      call you Henrietta. You're
      so cool. And so are you,
      Bray. You know that?

DAL arrives, panicked.


                    DAL
      Lex is in trouble. He needs
      some help!

AT THE ANTIDOTE STALL

LEX is in a huge brawl. Although he is
giving a good account of himself like the
street fighter he is - he is getting badly
beaten by some members of the LOCOS.

And JACK is trying to pull them away.

                    JACK
          He's had enough! Please!
          You're going to kill him!
          Come on! He won't take much
          more!!!

A LOCO spins, hurls JACK to the ground
and we can see TRUDY, EDEN, SALENE, and
AMBER approaching in the background from
different directions.

JACK climbs unsteadily to his feet and
cringes as a LOCO raises a pole, ready
to strike.

DAL, MOUSE, SAMMY and BRAY arrive. BRAY
quickly steps in, twists, leaps, kicks,
disarming the LOCO about to strike JACK,
the pole hurling from the LOCO'S grip.

And then with a series of impressive
martial arts moves, BRAY deals with the
other LOCOS and it doesn't take long for
all the LOCOS to disperse, not wishing to
get on the wrong side of THIS dude.

LEX tends his wounds, BRAY extends a hand
to help LEX up.

                    LEX
          Thanks. I owe you one.

EDEN, TRUDY, SALENE and AMBER arrive.

                    AMBER
        What happened?!

It's not easy for JACK and DAL to own up
- but they do.

                    DAL
        We were trying to trade
        mint water. As a cure for
        the virus. And some of the
        Locos found out.


                    AMBER
        How could you?!


                    LEX
        Yeah, I'm fine, thanks. I'll
        just stand and bleed to
        death. With all my wounds.
        Don't worry about me!


                    AMBER
        You brought it on yourself.
        'Mint water'? No one should
        ever try and con a Loco.
        You should know that.


                    LEX
        That's a comfort.


                    AMBER
        Can someone help Lex? Get
        him cleaned up?

EDEN, SALENE are already onto it. DAL
pours water, TRUDY soaks cloths and
passes them to EDEN and SALENE, wiping
at LEX'S wounds.

> AMBER
> What made you think you'd
> get away with it?

> JACK
> Technically ... we didn't.

> AMBER
> Though you got part of it
> right. If you and your team
> could ever develop one,
> Jack, it'd be a powerful
> currency.

> JACK
> That's for sure. We were
> offered all kinds of
> things. You name it. One
> girl was ... well ... she
> ... was thinking about ...
> all kinds of things.

He can't bring himself to say sex but
AMBER has an idea, casts him a look. He
fakes an uneasy smile and backs away.

> JACK
> I'll go and check out all

                    JACK (cont'd)
        the inventory of stuff.
        (suddenly to get in the
        good books) Filtered rain
        water did well.


                    AMBER
        Glad to hear it.

She considers JACK who turns, heads
quickly to the stall, eager to get away
and AMBER sighs to herself, bewildered
with it all.


                    BRAY
        So ... how are all the
        negotiations going?


                    AMBER
        We're taking a break. And
        have agreed to come back to
        it. Only problem though is
        - Zoot seems to have gone
        missing. Just hope a double
        cross isn't going down.


INT. FLAME'S INNER SANCTUM. PRIVILEGED
RESORT. NIGHT.

Flaming torches on the walls cast looming
shadows. FLAME stands gazing absently
at his multiple reflections in a wall of
mirrors, lost in thought, playing his
guitar - awesome wailing riffs.

Doors burst open. HARMONY, OX, and the
SECURITY burst in, hurl a hooded, rope-
bound and gagged FIGURE to the ground.

FLAME doesn't even turn. Or seem to
bother to look, take any notice. Just
keeps wailing those guitar riffs.

But we can see in the reflection HARMONY
yanking off the hood revealing ZOOT, as
he is forced down to his knees.

                    HARMONY
          Well, you asked for him,
          Flame - and here he is.
          Zoot, the very man himself.
          And we didn't even have to
          trade. Anything. So ...
          slave camps?

Still FLAME ignores Zoot, everyone
else. Just keeps wailing those riffs,
preoccupied, gazing absently at his
reflection as if lost in a different world.

                    HARMONY
          Flame? Look, I brought you
          Zoot. As planned. What do
          you want done with him?

FLAME still doesn't look at ZOOT, just
his own reflection.

                    FLAME
        I want him bathed and
        cleansed. Then I'll 'deal'
        with him. After my practice
        session.

INT. SHOPPING MALL. NIGHT.

TRUDY is breast feeding the BABY in the
bedding department, SALENE, EDEN, AMBER,
sitting on some beds nearby.

                    SALENE
        Maybe the Guardian was
        lying? About Zoot?

                    AMBER
        Could be ... there again
        ....?

                    TRUDY
        He wouldn't need to use
        that as a tactic to delay
        the negotiations. I mean,
        he could come up with all
        kinds of reasons.

                    AMBER
        With Zoot and the Guardian
        you just never know what
        you're dealing with.

DAL and JACK arrive.

                    TRUDY
        Any luck?


                    JACK
        No. We've double checked his
        room. All over the mall.
        Again. Looked - everywhere!


                    AMBER
        Odd. For Bray to ALSO
        suddenly go AWOL.


                    EDEN
        Was only a question of
        time. All free spirits move
        on.


                    TRUDY
        I wouldn't be so sure. He
        promised he would stay for
        a while, Eden ... and Bray?
        He's solid. Someone you CAN
        trust.


A sustained os wailing SCREAM echoing
through the mall.


                    AMBER
        What's going on!


IN THE FOOD HALL

MOUSE is hysterical. And SAMMY as well.
The RATS arrive in growing panic and

concern.

> AMBER
> What happened?!

> MOUSE
> Poor Henrietta!!!

> AMBER
> Take Mouse and Sammy to
> their quarters, try and
> calm them down.

MOUSE hands AMBER a plate of bones, then EDEN leads a sobbing, VERY distraught MOUSE and SAMMY away.

AMBER glares at LEX, sitting at a table licking his fingers, emitting a huge belch.

> AMBER
> You didn't?!

> LEX
> Don't look at me like that!
> I was hungry!

> AMBER
> You're disgusting!!!

> LEX
> And after the hassle at the
> Gathering, reckon I

                    LEX (cont'd)
          deserved a treat. Henrietta
          was the best meal I've had.
          In ages!


                    AMBER
          Pathetic!!!


                    LEX
          What the hell is wrong?!
          After the amount of people
          who have been wiped out.
          It's just one more death.
          And only a goddamn chicken!

He burps again. AMBER, SALENE and TRUDY
glare at him in horror, disbelief - and
he yells after them as they storm away.

                    LEX
          No hope for a new generation
          of Mall Rats if kids like
          Mouse don't toughen up.
          She needs to get over it.
          What's the big deal?!

EXT. FOREST NIGHT.

A BOWIE KNIFE cutting sections of rope
and vines.

REVEAL BRAY

moving furtively through the darkness in a

forest area, tying vines, rope, attaching them to trees bordering a track.

INT. FLAME'S INNER SANCTUM. PRIVILEGED RESORT. NIGHT.

ZOOT now robed but still gagged, hands bound, is thrown by OX to the floor.

HARMONY watches, fascinated as FLAME sips on his Kava, crosses and gazes down at ZOOT.

> FLAME
> Zoot. The Mighty warrior
> Zoot. You know, you could
> have even been a candidate
> to be Privileged. Because as
> well as being so powerful,
> legendary, I couldn't help
> but notice at the Gathering
> that you are also ...
> strangely quite beautiful.

EXT. BORDERING THE PRIVILEGED RESORT. NIGHT.

The resort, bathed in moonlight, illuminated by flaming torches.

And we find BRAY taking cover in the shadows, checking out GUARDS passing on patrol.

INT. FLAME'S INNER SANCTUM. PRIVILEGED
RESORT. NIGHT.

FLAME circling ZOOT, flicking Kava from
his bowl as if anointing him.

ZOOT flinches with each zap of liquid.

FLAME smiles but it's ice cold, his
delivery laced in mock concern - but
manic.

> FLAME
> Oh, you don't like that,
> Zoot? Shame. You see, Kava
> can take you to places -
> just like music - you've
> never been before. In a
> journey of discovery that
> will blow your mind! Love
> it. And it'll love you back.
> Hate it and ... well ...
> hate is such an interesting
> emotion I've learned to
> discover since the darkness
> descended.

He sips more of the liquid, sniffs at it,
savors it, then gazes absently, coldly at
ZOOT again.

> FLAME
> And tonight, mighty Zoot
> ... you will discover

                    FLAME (cont'd)
        what it is like to BE
        Privileged. Because the god
        Flame himself, yes me, will
        drain you of every drop of
        blood and suck out your
        very soul! (to OX) Restrain
        him!


EXT. PRIVILEGED RESORT. NIGHT.

BRAY crossing carefully to a compound
where he starts to siphon gas from
vehicles.

INT. FLAME'S INNER SANCTUM. PRIVILEGED
RESORT. NIGHT.

ZOOT'S EYES wild with terror, his cries
of pain sounding even more anguished by
his gag as FLAME leaps on ZOOT'S back,
yanks at ZOOT'S hair, drawing his head
back - and is in danger of choking him.

But it seems to only excite FLAME more.
He starts kissing, then biting at the
back of ZOOT'S neck.

HARMONY and OX watching, surprised, and
as fascinated by it as they are disturbed.

EXT. PRIVILEGED. RESORT. NIGHT.

BRAY moves quietly, stealthily, keeping
an eye on other GUARDS who pass while he

pours a long line of fuel, emptying the entire canister.

INT. FLAME'S INNER SANCTUM. PRIVILEGED RESORT. NIGHT.

FLAME almost like a wild animal, is losing control, and he starts sucking, drawing blood which over spills onto FLAMES'S own face amidst the sweat, the drooling, while feverishly caressing ZOOT'S body and groin.

OX and HARMONY watch, spell bound, unable to take their eyes off it all.

FLAME groaning now in a manic frenzy, intensity, ZOOT'S horrific distress and cries seemingly fueling FLAME'S cruel, sadistic urge as he bites ZOOT'S neck again. Again.

And FLAME is finally almost GAGGING himself, unable to cope with an overload of sheer primitive, deviant pleasure as he tears at the skin, sucks and swallows more blood.

ZOOT spins, the momentum hurling FLAME to the ground. OX steps and unleashes a kick into ZOOT'S groin, doubling him.

HARMONY watches, disturbed but it is unclear if it is by what she has just witnessed, or through sympathy for a distraught ZOOT lying collapsed on the floor?

Or more by FLAME climbing to his feet and starting to laugh, manically, as he wipes, licks, tastes ZOOT'S blood in his mouth while gazing at his multitude of reflections in the wall of mirrors.

Reflecting seemingly endless multiple images of swirling flames from the torches –

And FLAME himself as if he is the devil in hell.

EXT. PRIVILEGED RESORT. NIGHT.

GUARDS pass and we find BRAY moving through the shadows to the main resort entrance.

INT. FLAME'S INNER SANCTUM. PRIVILEGED RESORT. NIGHT.

FLAME downs more Kava, sinks slowly to his knees, his manic laughter subsiding - and he breaks down in uncontrollable sobbing, wracking, heaving sobs, gazing intently, hallucinating at his reflection.

HARMONY

You ... OK?

FLAME

Why shouldn't I be?! I'm

FLAME (cont'd)
Flame, right! Well?!!! Or
the devil???!!! Who?!!!

He hurls the bowl in fury at the wall of
mirrors which shatters.

Reflecting even more multiple fragmented
images, increasing  FLAME'S distress as
he gazes at himself, blood oozing out of
his mouth - and at ZOOT behind, amidst
the flaming torches.

HARMONY
You're a god, Flame,
worshipped by all!

FLAME
Zoot! He's the devil,
Harmony. Bad blood! Get rid
of him! NOW! Get him out of
my sight!!!

HARMONY
What do you want done with
him - slave camps?

FLAME
No! No way. No. No. No. No.
No.  Not after all he's
done ...

He staggers, turns, gazes down at ZOOT -
and his face is twisted in a mixture of

confusion, fear, rage and steaming hate.

>                    FLAME
>                 (intones)
>          Oh, mighty Zoot! I commit
>          you, as the god Flame,
>          to go before the Supreme
>          Council. To be tried for
>          being impure of blood and
>          soul! And for being ...
>          EVIL!

OX and HARMONY exchange an uneasy glance
as FLAME erupts in manic laughter again.

The he turns and gazes at the multiple
reflections of himself and ZOOT amidst the
swirling flames.

>                    FLAME
>          No room for you in
>          Privileged heaven, Devil,
>          Zoot, my friend. You're
>          going back to hell!!!

INT. HALLWAY. PRIVILEGED RESORT. NIGHT.

A line of eerie, white robed, hooded
members of the PRIVILEGED SUPREME COUNCIL
pass, carrying candles and all chanting
an ominous mantra.

But the LAST in line disappears amidst
a barely perceptible groan, yanked from

the shadows through the doorway into a room.

EXT. THE MAIN PRIVILEGED RESORT. NIGHT.

The pounding of drums. ZOOT, his hands bound by rope, is led before the assembled TRIBE and hooded, robed SUPREME COUNCIL.

> HARMONY
> Flame recommends no mercy
> for the Warrior Zoot
> standing before you. And
> the penalty of death! What
> is your recommendation,
> Supreme Council?

The SUPREME COUNCIL chant in unison.

> SUPREME COUNCIL
> Stoning! ... Stoning!!
> ...Stoning!!!

The TRIBE erupt into a chilling frenzied shrieking, all ululating in unison, and HARMONY yells above it all.

> HARMONY
> Any Tribal brother or sister
> who has been affected by
> Zoot - or the Locos - now
> has a chance to settle the
> score. And collect a stone.

A MEMBER OF THE ROBED SUPREME COUNCIL, crosses, lifts a stone.

> HARMONY
> Ah, a real honor to have
> a member of the Supreme
> Council, Tribal brothers
> and sisters, cast the very
> first stone! Thank you,
> exalted one, for giving us
> a start.

But rather than at ZOOT - the Council MEMBER smashes the stone into the face of a GUARD nearby, and we reveal -

BRAY

In disguise as the hooded MEMBER, now cutting the ropes binding a very surprised ZOOT with his bowie knife, Privileged SECURITY quickly moving in.

> BRAY
> Follow me! Move!

FEATURING HARMONY

Yelling instructions over all the frenzy, the pounding of the drums.

> HARMONY
> Go after them?! Don't let

                  HARMONY (cont'd)
            them get away!!

HARMONY and the Tribal WARRIOR GUARD run
flat out in pursuit.

BRAY AND ZOOT

In full flight running for their lives,
both capable warriors, taking out any in
their path.

BRAY yanking a flaming torch from the
hands of one GUARD which he hurls -

IGNITING A WALL OF FIRE

Providing enough of a barrier to block
some but not all of the masses of the
gathering TRIBE in pursuit.

THE CHASE

ZOOT and BRAY running flat out.

Privileged WARRIORS are gaining.

BRAY and ZOOT scaling a fence, leaping to
the ground.

And exchanging blows with GUARDS who
converge near the vehicle compound but
are quickly taken out.

BRAY and ZOOT keep going, pushing
themselves to the limit, breathless,

exhausted but finding the will to carry on.

But GUARDS are almost on them now.

BRAY and ZOOT, running in full flight towards the dune buggy.

                    BRAY
          Get in. Move it, move it!

They leap into the buggy. BRAY starts the engine, accelerates, heading towards a group of Privileged GUARDS who scatter -

As the Buggy recedes away -

And rush to their own Tribe vehicles in the compound.

Some are out of gas, won't start (as a result of Bray emptying the tanks earlier).

But the deafening engine noises of a few motorcycles explode into action, as GUARDS speed off in pursuit.

EXT. FOREST. NIGHT.

BRAY and ZOOT clinging as the Dune buggy hurls through the darkness, along a track in the forest.

The motor cycles in pursuit, gaining -

fast.

ZOOT AND BRAY TRAVELLING

Steal looks behind, then BRAY spins the
steering wheel.

                    BRAY
          Better hold on tight!

THE DUNE BUGGY

Speeds off the track, through trees,
avoiding the area we saw Bray in earlier.

BRAY spins the wheel again, back on the
track.

The buggy hits an incline, is slightly
airborne, hurls through the air, then
lands, skids, continues speeding away.

THOSE IN PURSUIT

Are caught by the trap Bray set, not
exactly garroted by the ropes and vines
hanging taut, suspended between the
trees, but are stopped dead.

The GUARDS are thrown from their
MOTORCYCLES which careen out of control,
twisting, turning through the air, gas
tanks igniting as they land.

Gigantic swirling FLAMES illuminating

the darkness and forest which explodes
in a mammoth FIREBALL.

EXT. LOOTED SHOPPING MALL. NIGHT.

The dune buggy draws to a stop. BRAY and
ZOOT leap out, cross to the sewer man
hole cover.

                    ZOOT
          Owe you, man. Big time.


                    BRAY
                  (Cold)
          You owe me nothing. Ever.


                    ZOOT
          By ever you can't mean
          forever, Bray.

BRAY casts him a look.

                    ZOOT
          Appreciate you being there.
          And it's war with the
          Privileged. For the Locos,
          for sure. I also 'owe'
          Flame, I'm telling you.
          Piece of scum!

BY THE MANHOLE COVER WHICH OPENS

Revealing AMBER and EDEN climbing through.
Astounded to see BRAY. And ZOOT. And they

cross briskly to them.

                    BRAY
          What are you both up to?


                    EDEN
          We were just about to head
          out on a reconnaissance
          mission.  To check the
          Locos' headquarters. For
          any sign (to Zoot) of you.


                    AMBER
          And we should be the ones
          asking the questions, Bray,
          because I'd say you've got
          some explaining to do!

She and EDEN follow BRAY and ZOOT heading
towards the man hole cover.

                    AMBER
          What happened?


                    ZOOT
          'Someone' gave me a love
          bite. Now they're going to
          know the meaning of - hate!

He dabs at the wound in his neck with a
piece of torn cloth and EDEN and AMBER
exchange glances in confusion and concern.

                    AMBER
      What are you talking about?


                    BRAY
      Zoot needed some help-


                    AMBER
      He's a Loco -


                    BRAY
      Back off, Amber! I'm not
      in any mood to hear any
      lectures from you -


                    AMBER
      What, you go AWOL, then
      just show up out of the
      blue. With Zoot. And expect
      no-one's going to ask for
      an explanation?!


                    ZOOT
      Better tell her, Bray.


                    BRAY
      OK. You want an explanation?
      You got it.


They stop and EDEN and AMBER are astounded
by the revelation.


                    BRAY
      You're always on about the

                    BRAY (cont'd)
          best way of securing the
          future. But that isn't just
          down to any differences
          between Tribes, Amber.
          This is about taking the
          first step to build a REAL
          future. Through a father
          meeting ... his son.

INT. LOOTED SHOPPING MALL. NIGHT.

We are in the food hall, illuminated by
candles. All the RATS (except the younger
ones) are watching ZOOT proudly, gently
cradling his BABY son.

                    ZOOT
          Got a name yet?


                    LEX
                   (Ice)
          How about Zoot Junior?


                    AMBER
          Don't go there, Lex.


                    TRUDY
          No, I haven't thought of a
          name.


                    ZOOT
          One day you might grow up

>           ZOOT (cont'd)
> to be a mighty warrior,
> won't you, eh? Yeah, Zoot
> might be a good choice of
> name.

LEX casts him a look. It was meant not as
a suggestion but an insult.

>           AMBER
> Why didn't you say anything,
> Trudy? I had no idea you
> were together.

>           TRUDY
> We weren't. For long. And
> I didn't exactly feel good
> about broadcasting to
> everyone and anyone about
> being dumped by the leader
> of the Locos. Even if it
> WAS probably the best thing
> to move on.

ZOOT hands the BABY back to TRUDY

>           ZOOT
> You ok? (she nods) So a
> Mall Rat, eh?

>           LEX
> No...

He sighs and doesn't pursue it as AMBER

flashes him a look - then she considers
BRAY.

> AMBER
> You obviously knew. About
> all this. Why didn't YOU
> say anything?

> BRAY
> It's no-one's business.

> AMBER
> No. But in this case it's
> a little different. And I
> think you SHOULD have said.
> You as well, Trudy.

> BRAY
> Not everything in life can
> ever be so black and white
> as you try to make out,
> Amber -

> AMBER
> I ... we... trusted you -

> BRAY
> And as leader of this Tribe
> you'd do yourself - and
> everyone - a big favor to
> remember that.

                    AMBER
I'm not going to sit and be
lectured by you!

                     LEX
No, you go for it, Bray -

                    AMBER
You're defending him now?!
Just because he helped you
out of a scrap - he's now
your best 'buddy pal'?
That's pathetic, Lex. Talk
about changing like night
and day. Now THAT'S black
and white!

                    BRAY
I just think you've got to
keep an open mind, Amber.
Or it can be a bit much at
times.

                    AMBER
And you can save the
insults!

                    BRAY
I'm just trying to make you
see that complications DO
exist in life, Amber. They
might never be that easy to
explain, let alone be

                    BRAY (cont'd)
understood ... but you've
just got to accept that
they're still there!!

                    LEX
I agree! Nice one.

                    AMBER
Oh, give it a break, Lex!

                    EDEN
I think everyone should try
and calm down. Not good
Karma to argue about all
this.

                    ZOOT
I'd better leave you guys
to it and make a move.

He strokes the BABY'S cheek, then
considers TRUDY.

                    ZOOT
Keep in touch, Babe. I'd
like to always know how
both of you are doing.

                    LEX
Wait a minute. You just
don't think you're -
leaving?

                    ZOOT
     I wasn't figuring on staying!


                    LEX
     Oh, you're staying -


                    AMBER
     What?!


                    LEX
     But not to play 'Daddy'
     with that half breed kid -


                    TRUDY
     Don't call my baby that!


                    LEX
     That's what it is! And
     what are you figuring on
     doing, Zoot ... taking 'it
     fishing', or teaching it all
     about Power and Chaos, how
     to carry out even more war
     crimes?

ZOOT steps forward to challenge LEX.


                    BRAY
     That's enough! Back off!
     Both of you!!!


                    AMBER
     I'm not exactly a 'fan'

                    AMBER (cont'd)
          of the Locos either - but
          Zoot's hardly guilty of any
          war crimes -


                    LEX
          Yeah, well, that's for a
          jury to decide. Bray's
          right. You're always on your
          high horse about stuff.
          Like a justice system. Now
          we can put it to the test.


                    AMBER
          It would be up to ALL the
          Tribes, Lex. Not just the
          Mall Rats to decide if
          Zoot's guilty of anything -


                    LEX
          From the run-ins with the
          Locos I've had - I got all
          the evidence I need. And I
          say - let's lock him up!

He grabs ZOOT.


                    ZOOT
          Get your hands off me!

He slams a fist into LEX'S gut which hurls
him to the ground, then LEX stands and
squares up to ZOOT.

                    BRAY
      That's enough, guys!

                    LEX
      No! If he wants to show how
      tough he really is when
      he's not surrounded by all
      his Loco warriors - bring
      it on!


He leaps at ZOOT. And they engage in a
huge fight which over spills -

TO THE BALCONY

Of the food hall, the RATS following
as LEX and ZOOT trade furious, vicious
blows.

BRAY steps between them to try and break
it up, yanking ZOOT away, then pushing
LEX back who stumbles to the floor.

ZOOT leaps to strike another blow. LEX
stands and amidst a sustained scream -
nooooooo -

ZOOT

Is propelled by the momentum over a
balcony, lands with a sickening THUD ...
and lays motionless several floors below
in the square.

DOWN IN THE SQUARE

The RATS race down the escalator, cross
to ZOOT. Silence descends. JACK feels for
a pulse, then shakes his head.

> JACK
>
> He's dead!

BRAY crouches by the body of ZOOT as
the other RATS exchange uneasy glances,
ominous realization setting in.

> JACK
>
> Man, now you're going to
> have a hell of a price on
> your head, Lex.

> SALENE
>
> It was self defence.

> AMBER
>
> I hope the Locos can
> understand that.

> LEX
>
> Hey, can you imagine? The
> reputation on the street?
> Gonna be awesome ... me
> ... the dude who took out
> Zoot!

                    AMBER
        It's nothing to be 'proud'
        of, Lex. And all the Rats
        ... we're all vulnerable -

DAL indicates BRAY crouched, distraught
and starting to sob quietly as he cradles
ZOOT'S face in his hands and draws him to
his chest.

                    DAL
        What's all that about?

He exchanges dumbfounded glances with
AMBER and all the RATS.

Then TRUDY sighs, a profound sadness
in her eyes which fill with tears, and
although she maintains great dignity -
she can hardly contain the emotion.

                    TRUDY
        As well as being the father
        of my child - Zoot ... He's
        also the estranged brother
        of Bray. Once known in the
        old world ... as Martin.

INT. BRAY'S QUARTERS. SHOPPING MALL. DAY.

AMBER enters a furniture store. She is
wearing black feathers in her hair, her
make up and lipstick, also black.

AMBER
We're all ready, Bray. If
you are?

BRAY nods. He is sitting on a bed placing
the last feathers into a cloak. Other
black feathers are intertwined in his
hair. He also has black war paint streaked
across his face.

And he looks magnificent as he stands and
throws the impressive cloak around his
shoulders.

EXT. SUBURBS. DAY.

All RATS are present as the funeral
procession makes its way in SILENCE
through the deserted, ghostly suburban
streets.

As with AMBER and BRAY, all the RATS are
also adorned in black make up, lipstick,
feathers.

BRAY is leading the procession, walking
ahead of the dune buggy - now a make-
shift cortege.

On which ZOOT'S body is laid out, not in
a casket but on a bed of feathers, eyes
closed, arms crossed.

TRUDY follows BRAY ahead of the cortege,
BABY in arms and all other RATS remain by

the side or behind.

INT. HOUSE. SUBURBIA. DAY.

Two ravaged, filthy looking scavenging STRAYS in a looted, decaying house peek, stealing frightened, wary looks through the windows, intrigued –

At the funeral PROCESSION passing.

EXT. BEACH. DAY.

ZOOT is placed into a funeral boat, a small wooden row boat.

The sounds of a gentle wind, waves lapping ashore and sudden flare of a cloth-bound torch which is lit, seem to punctuate the elemental atmosphere.

The RATS watch as BRAY, holding the torch, glances at the body of ZOOT.

> BRAY
> I know how you all feel
> about Zoot. I don't agree
> with pretty much of
> anything he and the Locos
> do. But in the old world,
> I can tell you that Martin
> and I, we were as close as
> any brothers can be. Two
> brothers. Who became two
> warriors. And chose a

                    BRAY (cont'd)
          different path. Somewhere
          along the way maybe we just
          ... LOST our way. Like so
          many seem to have done these
          days. But as we commit
          Martin to his final journey,
          I do so honouring those who
          have gone before. Before
          the darkness arrived. His
          Parents - my parents. Our
          Mother ... And our Father
          ...

His voice cracks with emotion and all the
RATS are affected, even LEX.

                    BRAY
          In this world ... Zoot would
          want to be honoured and
          remembered as a warrior.
          And he was certainly that.
          Even if you disagreed with
          all he might have stood
          for. So today I ask you
          to join with me, as he
          takes the final step on his
          journey and embarks upon
          a new one ... in the hope
          that he finds peace along
          the way...

BRAY torches the boat, which burns.

All RATS watch as the burning boat is cast off in FLAMES and heads to the distant Sun setting across the darkening, stormy horizon of the sea.

EXT. THE CITY SQUARE. NIGHT.

A deafening crack of thunder, lightning streaking across the night sky.

The fanatical GUARDIAN addressing the assembled LOCOS, whipped into a frenzied shrieking as more lightning zig zags all around.

                    GUARDIAN
          It is a sign! From the
          great one! Mighty Zoot! And
          he WILL be avenged!!!

INT. LOOTED SHOPPING MALL. NIGHT.

BRAY restless, unable to sleep. Suddenly opens his eyes, aware of a presence.

And we reveal through the darkness - a robe falling to the floor.

Then the beautiful, naked body of EDEN is visible, crawling into bed.

                    BRAY
          Eden ... what are you
          doing?

                    EDEN
          I want to give you some
          comfort.


                    BRAY
          Look, it's not that I don't
          think you're attractive.
          Because you are.


                    EDEN
          Then hold me. Close.


She kisses him. But he gently pushes her
away.


                    BRAY
          Eden, I appreciate the
          thought. But, no ....


                    EDEN
          Some advice then. The fates
          of you, me, Zoot, the Rats,
          all Tribes are intertwined.
          Whatever happens is for a
          reason. In the end.


                    BRAY
          Somehow I think all that
          has happened is due to
          something more than
          destiny, Eden.

                    EDEN
        No. And no-one can change
        destiny. So don't even try.
        As with your brother ...
        you will never discover
        new horizons without the
        courage to lose sight of
        the shore. Learn to let go,
        Bray.

LEX arrives.

                    LEX
        So that's where you are,
        Eden. Suspected as much.

                    EDEN
        What's the matter? Has
        Salene finally come to her
        senses?

                    LEX
        Just wanted to check on
        Bray. If you're ok? But if
        you're busy -

                    BRAY
        No. Eden was just leaving.

                    LEX
        Hey, not a problem. I'm
        cool with it. Could be a
        good initiation. Wish I had

                    LEX (cont'd)
        it when I joined.


                    BRAY
        I haven't said anything
        about joining the Tribe,
        Lex.


                    LEX
        Well, think about it.
        Because I have. And I
        reckon you might have a lot
        to offer.


                    EDEN
        I would agree with that.

She slips out of bed, places her robe on.


                    EDEN
        If you change your mind,
        Bray, you know where to find
        me.


                    LEX
        In my bed?


                    EDEN
        I don't belong to just any
        man, Lex. Or anyone for
        that matter. Only myself.

And she leaves. LEX considers BRAY and

it's not easy for him to say but he does.

> LEX
>
> About Zoot. I ... didn't
> mean for it to turn out
> that way.

> BRAY
>
> I know that, Lex.

> LEX
>
> What you were saying at his
> funeral ... it ... well,
> it kind of got to me if you
> must know ... and I just
> wanted YOU to know that I
> had you figured all wrong.
> And I'm sorry. Respect,
> man.

> BRAY
>
> Same, Lex. Thanks.

They slap hands, then grip hard in the
ensuing handshake.

EXT. PRIVILEGED RESORT. NIGHT.

GUARDS stand aside, raise a barrier as a
RIDER on a horse gallops into the resort.

The RIDER dismounts, crosses briskly to
the main compound.

INT. FLAME'S INNER SANCTUM. PRIVILEGED
RESORT. NIGHT.

The ANDROGYNOUS SERVANTS bathe the hands
of FLAME, paint his nails. HARMONY enters.

> HARMONY
> A messenger has just
> arrived with news from an
> informant in Sector 9.

> FLAME
> Reliable?

> HARMONY
> Wrong time. Right place.
> And he didn't want to die.
> I'd say it was pretty
> reliable.

> FLAME
> What's the situation?

> HARMONY
> Seems Zoot has been taken
> out. By the Mall Rats. And
> you know what that means?

> FLAME
> War?

> HARMONY
> You can bet on it! Could

>                    HARMONY (cont'd)
>           be the right time for the
>           Privileged to plan on
>           making a move. And strike.

>                    FLAME
>           Do it!

EXT. ROOFTOP OF THE MALL. NIGHT.

AMBER gazes out across the night sky,
suburbia, the dark silhouette of the city
visible beyond in the distance.

A BEAT, then BRAY arrives.

>                    BRAY
>           Couldn't sleep either, eh?

>                    AMBER
>           Hopefully not. My turn on
>           the rota. Guard duty.

She smiles and BRAY smiles despite himself
too.

>                    BRAY
>           I can take over if you
>           want. No point us both
>           losing sleep.

>                    AMBER
>           No, I'm fine. Thanks anyway.
>           (a beat). I love to come

                    AMBER (cont'd)
up here. At night. Look out
across all the sectors. It
helps me think of what once
was, how it is now, how it
could be.


                    BRAY
Sure is peaceful.


                    AMBER
But for how long? We need
to try and arrange a
meeting. With the Guardian.
Explain what happened.

BRAY nods. An uneasy silence again, both
looking out at the night. Then they both
overlap.


                    BRAY
Listen Amber, I've been
thinking -


                    AMBER
Bray, I just want to say -


                    BRAY
After you.


                    AMBER
I'm sorry about your
brother. And for giving you

                    AMBER (cont'd)
a hard time.


                    BRAY
It's me who should
apologize.


                    AMBER
No. You're right. I have
to try and keep more of an
open mind. If I have any
hope of introducing any new
charter. Bill of rights.
Otherwise the Rats might
never bring about any real
change.


                    BRAY
No-one should ever
apologize for trying to do
that, Amber.


                    AMBER
What about for losing hope?
This new crazy world we all
live in seems so out of
control at times.


                    BRAY
Don't lose hope. You should
feel proud. You're doing a
great job. I just hope ...
that YOU don't change.

AMBER looks at BRAY and they exchanges glances for a long beat. Then he draws her closer and they kiss, gently at first, then with increasing passion.

EXT. CITY STREETS. DAY.

Lined with LOCOS shrieking wildly, faces streaked with paint, some pounding war drums.

And we find BRAY, AMBER, EDEN AND SALENE amongst a delegation of RATS with a white flag of truce heading into the city square.

EXT. CITY SQUARE. DAY.

The GUARDIAN is cold as the RAT delegation arrive.

> GUARDIAN
> You've all got to be very
> brave.  Or very stupid
> to come into the Locos'
> sector, especially after
> what happened.

> AMBER
> We HAD to, Guardian. Not
> just for the sake of the
> Rats but the Locos, all the
> Tribes.

                    BRAY
Whatever you might have
heard, Lex and the Mall
Rats are innocent. It's
true there was a fight ...
but it could have as easily
been Lex who died ... it
was an accident.


                    EDEN
And in case you didn't know
... Bray is the brother of
Zoot. He has forgiven. And
so should you.


                    AMBER
The Privileged are the
real threat, Guardian. And
they'll only benefit from
any kind of conflict between
the Locos and the Rats.


                    GUARDIAN
The brother of Zoot?


                    AMBER
Blood brothers. And you
know what Zoot would do.
He would never give the
Privileged a chance to
divide and rule. With only
one result. Slavery and
oppression of ALL Tribes.

                    AMBER (cont'd)
          Including the Locos.


                    BRAY
          The battle lines must be
          drawn, Guardian. And we
          need to know if we can look
          to the Locos to be by our
          side.

The GUARDIAN nods.

INT. FOOD HALL. LOOTED SHOPPING MALL.
DAY.

All our regular older RATS are going over
strategy as JACK hands AMBER a sheet of
paper.

                    JACK
          We've made a list of all
          the logistics we need to
          go over. Behind the lines.
          After all - an army won't
          get very far without food,
          water, supplies. We'll also
          need a unit of medics ...
          Don't think we've forgotten
          anything.


                    AMBER
          No. This is all very
          impressive. Well done.

                    JACK
          Better be. I had an Ace One
          Rating on War Lord.

                    BRAY
          Guys, I was also a
          fanatical gamer. Once. But
          you've got to realize that
          any success in this conflict
          isn't the same as topping
          the leader boards in the
          old world. We're living in
          a different world now - and
          are about to experience the
          real thing 'live' - not on
          a virtual reality online
          game.

The thought is both intriguing as well as
frightening to JACK, DAL and their team
of GEEKS.

                    BRAY
          We SHOULD look to the codes
          of Bushido though. But from
          Ancient times. The way of
          the warrior. Action. And
          reaction.

LEX moves condiments outlining his battle
plan.

                    LEX
I was thinking a column
of Tribe Circus here ...
backed up by the Locos and
then we might get a pincer
movement ...


                    AMBER
What do you think, Bray?


                    BRAY
I agree. Draw them in. Then
we can control the middle
and close in from each
side. But we've GOT to get
to the very top. To those
in command. Get to them.
Fast. If and when we take
them out. Action. Reaction.
That's where the battle
will be won. Or lost.


                    AMBER
We need an urgent call to
arms. Better spread the
word to all Tribes. In all
sectors!


EXT. ANOTHER SECTOR. DAY.

A huge bonfire stack is lit on the top of
a hill by a MEMBER of a TRIBE as the sun
sets.


                    190

EXT. YET ANOTHER SECTOR. NIGHT.

Other TRIBES, watching the fires in the far distance, then torching their own bonfire stacks to pass the message on, the mammoth flames raging high into the dark sky.

INT. TRUDY'S QUARTERS. LOOTED SHOPPING MALL. NIGHT.

The BABY is fast asleep in its crib.

BRAY in feathered warrior mode, his face streaked by paint, enters, checks the BABY. Then he unzips a pocket in his cloak, removes an old photograph of him with his brother and parents taken in happier times in the old world.

He traces one finger across the photograph, smiles slightly, sadly at past memories, then he places it by the side of the BABY in the crib.

And kisses one finger which he gently places on the BABY'S cheek.

IN THE MAIN SQUARE

MOUSE and SAMMY are role play fighting as BRAY crosses towards the food hall. MOUSE is desperate to proudly show BRAY her moves.

MOUSE
Hey, Bray. Me and Sammy
have  been training - look!

BRAY can't help but smile as the tiny
MOUSE turns from SAMMY and attacks BRAY,
swinging wildly, and he places one hand
on her head to keep her at bay.

BRAY
Careful now. Someone could
get hurt.

MOUSE
Yeah! Like The Privileged.
And when I get bigger -
they'll see what I can
REALLY do.

BRAY crouches down to her level.

BRAY
No, Mouse. This is all
about trying to make sure
that you or Sammy or ANY of
the younger ones NEVER have
to go through any of this
when they are older.

MOUSE
(disappointment)
Oh! ... You mean we can
never go to war?

                    BRAY
          Not if the Mall Rats or
          I can help it. Now while
          everyone else is away - you
          and Sammy need to help look
          out for Trudy and the baby.
          Can you do that for me?


                    MOUSE
          OK.  We're all like a big
          family now, right?


                    BRAY
          Right.  And if anything
          happens to me - or anyone
          else - always remember
          that. We're all we've got.
          And we've got to look out
          for each other.


IN THE FOOD HALL

The eve of battle. Long lines of WARRIORS
in a queue. LEX, JACK, DAL, SALENE, and
TRUDY handing out an assortment of weapons
to the RAT and LOCO MILITIA. All the RATS
are in full warrior mode and attire.

BRAY arrives at a table nearby where EDEN
and AMBER are tying flags and banners to
long poles.

                    BRAY
          Ready?

                    AMBER
Just about.


                    EDEN
Just wish we could delay
... even twenty-four hours.
My chakras are out of
alignment.


                    AMBER
Well, I've never discounted
anything you ever say about
your 'feelings', Eden. But
it's not our call.


                    EDEN
Don't know what it is ...
but something is telling me
...


                    BRAY
All Tribes are mobilized.
And you can be sure the
Privileged will also be
gathering.


                    AMBER
We've got no choice, Eden.
If we're ever going to go -
it's got to be now.

EXT. HILLS. DAY.

A Tribal WARRIOR framed against the rising dawn sun high on a hill, blowing into a bull HORN ... a call to arms.

EXT. PANNING ACROSS THE CRESTS OF OTHER HILLS. DAY.

Pounding war drums, TRIBES with standard Flags and Banners fluttering in the winds, appearing over the ridge, marching on their way to battle, carrying pikes tagged with feathers, home made shields.

EXT. SEA. DAY.

WARRIORS in long, dug out canoes decorated with intimidating designs for war, also on their journey, frenzied chanting, paddling in unison.

EXT. FORESTS. DAY.

Another TRIBE marching through forests, some on horses, the faces of the animals also streaked with fierce war paint.

EXT. PLAINS. DAY.

The gathering hero FORCES marching, coming together across open fields, plains - the pine forests and mountains of the lands of the Privileged visible in the far distance.

And it is a breathtaking visual, a mixture of different cultures, colors and designs.

Not reminiscent of modern warfare in any way.

The base aesthetic is MORE like the clans at the battle of Culloden. But even that is a superficial comparison. This is all so strangely familiar, yet also looks like something we have NEVER seen before.

Most of the TRIBES are marching on foot. But some are on horseback, some even have wild looking dogs, snarling and straining on heavy chain leashes.

WARRIORS (and only a few) are in graffiti tagged vehicles, trucks, the hoods painted with frightening images, scowling faces, wild eyes, jaws of sharp teeth, all modified, like chariots with blades protruding.

And some are even sitting on motorized lawn mowers, tractors, tagged, streaked with war paint, long pole lances protruding.

Other WARRIORS are riding motorcycles and there is one coach - and amidst the tagging we are aware of the surreal sight of a red cross sign on this, the Tribes' hospital bus.

Anything and everything scavenged from society is almost used or worn - garbage can tin armor, twisted wires as hair extensions sprouting from welding masks, hockey masks.

Some inspired by the elemental, with feathers and war paint, look like a cross between the Apache and the Zulu. Others with animal skins and horns almost more like a cross between the Vikings, barbarians, and wild motorcycle gangs.

And we have already seen the ECOS and DEMON DOGS who now join the columns of the gathering hero FORCES.

But it is also the sounds that are just so striking, rousing. Beating drums. And pipes. Accompanying the frenzied cacophony of chanting of all the TRIBES.

FEATURING BRAY AND AMBER AND THE MALL RATS

Leading the assembled ARMY forming as a united force behind - and just ahead of the LOCOS, following the GUARDIAN in ZOOT'S police patrol car. The only Mall Rat vehicle is EDEN'S dune buggy, on which she is sitting on the hood, another WARRIOR driving.

The RATS look awesome. Faces streaked by war paint, feathers adorning their grungy clothes, hair, banners and flags fluttering in the wind, expressions set, determined, proud.

Now the faint sound of a distant guitar is suddenly audible amidst all the noise of the chanting, the pipes, and beating drums.

Which brings some unease, especially to SALENE, DAL and JACK and they swallow in nervous anticipation.

EXT. PINE FOREST. MOUNTAINS. DAY.

FLAME in the mountains, though this time not at the very peak.

He is head banging, back and forth, back and forth, playing a repetitive wailing note which reverberates all around, the sounds almost deafening amidst whistling feedback, his long blond hair blowing in the wind, framing the horrific site of his face - covered entirely in blood.

EXT. OUTER FRINGES OF THE PRIVILEGED COMPOUND. DAY.

HARMONY on a white stallion, the same lightning bolt tattooed on her face painted around the eye of the horse which even has the very same feathers as she does plaited in its beaded mane hair.

She is trotting slowly down the PRIVILEGED
front line as they prepare to move on
and into battle, though the DISCARDS are
being marshaled well in front, still
shackled, chained.

And the PRIVILEGED forces look so
intimidating, formidable, threatening
- especially the militia with their
tattooed faces. All are streaked with war
paint, horns, animal skins, shells, and
they seem as if they have been conjured
up from hell.

FLAME is visible on the Mountain ridge,
the rays of sun enshrining him like a
god, his repetitive wail of the guitar
whipping all into a frenzy and some are
also head banging as if lost in a private
reverie, a manic trance.

And we can hear the distant chanting,
pipes, pounding of the drums becoming
louder ... LOUDER -

As the Tribal armies approach closer ...
CLOSER.

HARMONY reigns her mount, yells above it
all, addressing the PRIVILEGED forces.

> HARMONY
> Remember the Discards will
> act as human shields. They
> will fall first. I will lead

```
        HARMONY (cont'd)
    the charge. And no way I'm
    going down!
```

The PRIVILEGED forces' chanting evolving
into a manic shriek as HARMONY whips them
into a frenzy.

```
            HARMONY
    Check out the god, Flame.
    His face is adorned with
    blood. The blood of all the
    infesting Rats we could
    find. That should remind you
    that defeat from the MALL
    RAT forces is not an option
    if we want to rid the lands
    of the impure.
```

The PRIVILEGED forces gaze up at FLAME
head banging on the mountain ridge and
even more start head banging themselves,
HARMONY yelling above it all.

```
            HARMONY
    So dig deep, my Tribal
    brothers and sisters. Seek
    courage - and if needs be
    lay down your lives for the
    cause. And generations will
    look back on this day of
    all days knowing that this
    is where it all began, when
    the ancestors of the pure
```

> HARMONY (cont'd)
> set about taking over the
> world, ridding it of any
> and all Mall Rats ... along
> with the scum of their
> vermin forces!

All erupt in even more of a frenzied
SHRIEKING, ULULATING, and start to march
into battle.

EXT. BATTLE FIELDS. DAY.

The pounding drums, pipes, wailing guitar,
chanting, the two ARMIES approaching
closer, closer - the divide narrowing.

And now nerves are starting to play a
part for other members of the RATS. With
even LEX and Amber and BRAY displaying
increasing unease in addition to DAL,
JACK and SALENE.

But EDEN is calming herself on the hood
of the dune buggy by adopting a lotus
position - and emits her mantra.

FEATURING BRAY

As both ARMIES suddenly slow the pace,
gaze across the narrowing distance at
each other.

The drums and pipes stop.

But not the distant wailing guitar, the sounds of the wind whipping up the fluttering banners, flags bringing a sense of peace in the tense silence.

Both ARMIES just seem to stare at each other. Sizing each other up across the divide.

BRAY swallows, takes a breath, gazes each side of him, behind, then ahead again, finally nodding.

                    BRAY
         It's on!

THE CHARGE INTO BATTLE

A deafening ROAR as both ARMIES, featuring the MALL RATS and PRIVILEGED, yell, running flat out towards each other - and into battle.

HUGE WOODED CATAPULT STRUCTURES

Are released by the PRIVILEGED back lines, hurling flaming balls of material now on fire through the air.

THE APPROACHING HERO FORCES FEATURING THE MALL RATS

As the balls of fire land, slightly disrupting the advance.

AND AS BOTH ARMIES ENGAGE

Mostly hand to hand combat, LEX is wielding a giant club bound by chains, taking anyone in his path out.

THE DISCARDS

Still bound, shackled, screaming helplessly, caught in the charge, unable to defend themselves as the ARMY of the hero forces pass, most featuring BRAY going round, avoiding them.

HARMONY

On her stallion, swinging a pike and cutting down her enemy.

PRIVILEGED BOWMEN

In the back lines drawing back their weapons and unleashing -

ARROWS

Arcing through the air, the sibilant sound audible above all the noise of the pounding drums, pipes, wailing guitar - and the battle.

THE HERO FORCES

Featuring SALENE in a column, crouching in a collective, raising shields for unified protection as the arrows fall but do not penetrate.

FEATURING JACK AND DAL

In another column, in the midst of battle as one arrow thwacks into the arm of DAL, piercing right through.

And JACK has lost it. He stands frozen in fear. He can't seem to do anything. Fight. Help. Even move. Just stares at the battle raging around him -

At DAL, gripping his arm -

As a huge PRIVILEGED WARRIOR approaches behind, raising a club to strike, but -

BRAY APPEARS IN FRAME

Takes out the WARRIOR with a spectacular martial art move, saving DAL.

FEATURING LEX

Swinging his club, backing up to give cover as BRAY rips a bit of cloth, quickly ties a tourniquet, yells at DAL over the NOISE of battle.

>                    BRAY
>           Better try and get behind
>           the lines. You're going to
>           need some treatment from
>           the medics, Dal!

And he draws the arrow from DAL'S arm.

JACK, sinks slowly to the ground. No, not by any enemy strike though he is close to having that happen ... he has fainted! So different to any war game he has ever played on any computer.

FLAME

On the ridge still head banging trancelike as he plays the same repetitive riff.

AMBER

Pushing on harder, harder, shielding enemy blows, fists, poles, pikes, knives, engaged in the thick of the hand to hand combat, suddenly gazes dumbfounded at

EDEN

Still in the lotus position on the dune buggy as the hero FORCES drive on and on through the thick of the battle.

And some of the PRIVILEGED enemy steal a confused glance. Mantra and Zen? Or is this chick a goddess, invincible - or just plain whacko?!

But EDEN uses her sixth sense, occasionally opens one eye to emit a lethal karate chop if anyone gets too close.

FEATURING THE MALL RATS

As the relentless drive of the hero FORCES is backing the PRIVILEGED toward their compound.

HARMONY

Reining her mount, yells above the frenzy of the battle.

>           HARMONY
>      Privileged Brothers and
>      Sisters, hold the lines!
>      Try and hold the lines!!
>      Stand firm!!!

Suddenly HARMONY is dragged from the horse -

By AMBER, the horse rearing up in panic onto its' hind legs. And wham! AMBER floors HARMONY with one punch.

AMBER

Gazes up at FLAME, then indicates to BRAY nearby.

>           AMBER
>      We've GOT to get to Flame!
>      He's the main one!

FEATURING BRAY

Twirling, kicking, in a series of awesome martial art movements, taking out any enemy in his path.

Then he runs, leaps onto the hood, roof of a vehicle to elevate him, then onto the patrol car and yells to the Guardian.

                    BRAY
          Time for phase two!

APPROACHING THE PRIVILEGED COMPOUND

As the patrol car smashes through barricades making way for our hero forces to advance even further.

BRAY glances up at FLAME on the mountain ridge, then his expression clouds as he notices -

A SPEAR

Hurling through the air and thudding into EDEN nearby.

BRAY

Aware that LEX is rushing to the aide of EDEN, leaps from the patrol car onto a passing motocross scrambling bike, knocking off the RIDER.

BRAY climbs to his feet, lifts the bike, mounts, kicks out at Privileged WARRIORS in his path as he accelerates away.

EXT. PINE FOREST. DAY.

BRAY speeding up a dirt track, through the pine forest ascending toward the mountain ridge.

EXT. RIDGE. MOUNTAINS. DAY.

FLAME still in a trance head banging back and forth, back and forth, repeating the wailing riff.

BRAY approaching from behind, leaps off the bike, rushes to FLAME, lunges and - yanks the guitar from him.

EXT. BATTLE FIELDS. DAY.

The PRIVILEGED gaze up, around as the guitar playing abruptly stops.

The sounds of the hero Tribal FORCES now dominating, the pounding drums, pipes, war cries of battle.

But still the whistling feedback reverberates around and around as if punctuating the anguish from the PRIVILEGED, slowly realizing that the battle is being lost.

EXT. RIDGE. MOUNTAINS. DAY.

FLAME still head bangs, rocking back and forth, yells at BRAY.

> FLAME
> Give me my guitar back!

> BRAY
> No way! Can't you see? It's finished! Over!

FLAME sinks slowly to his knees.

> FLAME
> In that case, do me a favor will you, dude? Drive the guitar right into my head. Over. And over. Yeah. Shatter my skull into millions of little pieces. My brain's gone. Can't take any more. But the guitar will take it. It's a Gibson 66 Les Paul ...

BRAY considers FLAME, who breaks into manic laughter and he taunts BRAY.

> FLAME
> What's the problem?! Don't you want the gig?! To take out a god?! Thought that would be so cool. Sure

```
            FLAME (cont'd)
       as hell would be for me.
       Then I can go to rock star
       heaven. In this godforsaken
       world only the good die
       young, man.
```

He gazes up at BRAY in sudden contempt, then snarls and screams in a petulant tantrum.

```
                FLAME
       Come on! Do it! Now!!! I
       want to be immortal!!!
```

Although BRAY has the opportunity to settle the score on behalf of his brother and is clearly desperate to take it -and for a second we even think he might - he denies himself.

FLAME suddenly cries out in sheer terror.

```
                FLAME
       Noooooooo!!!!!
```

BRAY is spinning with all his might and hurls -

THE GUITAR

Which twists, turns, falling through the air, amidst deafening feedback, breaking branches of pine trees in the forests below.

And we go into slow motion -

As the guitar lands, bounces on the ground, then settles. Intact. Least Flame got THAT right.

EXT. PRIVILEGED RESORT. DAY.

Peace in the aftermath of battle. PRIVILEGED being rounded up, DISCARD slaves unshackled, freed.

And we find DAL crouched by JACK outside the hospital bus.

DAL, himself with one arm in a sling, is holding some smelling salts with the other hand, under the nose of JACK, slapping his face.

> DAL
> Come on. Get a grip. All
> this fainting is starting
> to freak me out.

JACK opens his eyes weakly, tries to focus but quickly comes around when DAL announces the good news.

> DAL
> The Privileged have been
> defeated. We won!

                    JACK
          Awesome!- The whole THING
          was awesome.


                    DAL
          I wouldn't call it that.

He indicates, sadly.

FEATURING AMBER CROUCHED BY EDEN

BRAY, leading FLAME by a rope behind the
bike, dismounts, rushes to their side.
LEX also crossing to EDEN from WARRIORS
in the background visible leading FLAME
away with other PRISONERS.


                    BRAY
          How is she?

He crouches, AMBER shakes her head,
doesn't need to answer. From the blood
loss and EDEN being barely conscious -
it's clear it's not good.

But EDEN seems to know of BRAY'S presence,
that he is there, reaches out to clutch
at, to squeeze his hand - hard.

Then her grip fades as fast as her life
ebbs away.

And it is heartbreaking for AMBER to see
her best friend die in the arms of BRAY.
Ironic. Leaving AMBER left feeling guilty

that she ended up having the affection of
BRAY which EDEN had so longed for. And
LEX himself even wipes at a tear.

INT. LOOTED SHOPPING MALL. DAY.

TRUDY, with the BABY in her arms, crosses
through the furniture store to BRAY,
soaking his face in a bowl of water.

> TRUDY
>> Bray? I've been thinking.
>> Of a name. And well ... it
>> might be a nice idea to
>> call the baby after his
>> grandfather ... your Dad
>> and Zoot's - Martin.

> BRAY
>> Don't know about that, Trudy
>> - his name was Aubrey.

He smiles slightly and TRUDY does too,
not impressed at all.

> TRUDY
>> Might not be such a good
>> idea.

> BRAY
>> Don't feel bad. He never
>> liked the name either.
>> Always preferred his nick
>> name ... Abbe ... that's

BRAY (cont'd)
what my brother used to
call him when he was just
learning to talk ... it was
never Daddy ... always Abbe
... and it kind of stuck.

TRUDY
Abbe ... that's different
... yes, I like that.
Abbe. And if you've got no
objection -

BRAY
It would be an honour!

IN THE FOOD HALL

The TRIBES, featuring our MALL RATS, are
assembled EAGERLY watching as the LEADERS
sign papers.

AMBER
And if you can just sign
the treaty there on behalf
of the Locos, Guardian ...
that leaves me. And we're
done!

The GUARDIAN does this, then AMBER signs.

AMBER
Well - with the Privileged
disbanded and all Discards

214

                    AMBER (cont'd)
          set free ... I'd say we've
          all got something special
          to celebrate. Party time!

EXT. BEACH. DAY.

A spit roast feast, dancing, all the TRIBES
featuring the MALL Rats, celebrating.

AMBER, BRAY and TRUDY with the baby are
on a high sand dune. And AMBER addresses
the assembly who turn and gaze up at her.


                    AMBER
          Mall Rats ... fellow Tribes
          ... We're all at the
          beginning of something new
          here. Not the end. And I
          would like now to present
          someone who will know all
          about that in the future
          ... This is - Abbe ...

TRUDY passes the BABY to BRAY who raises
it to the ASSEMBLY below.


                    AMBER
          Check out not only the look
          of pride - but hope in the
          eyes of Abbe's mother,
          Trudy. Just like the eyes
          of ANY Mother for her
          child. But today that

          AMBER (cont'd)
hope should be shared by
all. For ALL tribes, ALL
people. And one day it
will be written, just like
in the ancient parables
and scriptures, that Abbe
on THIS day, even for one
brief shining moment, is
a savior heralding a new
and fair and just order.
For ALL tribes building a
better world from the ashes
of the old. To the future.
Our future.

The MALL RATS below, FEATURING LEX, JACK,
DAL, MOUSE, SALENE AND SAMMY, step and
chant along with the assembly of TRIBES.

Gazing up at AMBER, TRUDY, the BABY
being held aloft by BRAY - in a unison
of worship, Abbe Messiah, Abbe Messiah,
Abbe Messiah ....

                THE END

        OR IS IT JUST THE BEGINNING.

## Also available as paperback and eBook formats:

## Keeping The Dream Alive

### by

### Raymond Thompson.

*The fascinating inside story about the making of the cult television series, The Tribe.*

An intriguing memoir charting the life and times of how someone growing up on the wrong side of the tracks in a very poor working class environment in post-War Britain was able to journey to the glittering arena of Hollywood, providing an inspirational insight into how the one most likely to fail at school due to a special need battled and succeeded against all the odds to travel the world, founding and overseeing a prolific international independent television production company.

With humorous insight into the fertile imagination of a writer's mind, the book explores life away from the red carpet in the global world of motion pictures and television - and reveals the unique story of how the cult series 'The Tribe' came into being. Along with a personal quest to exist and survive amidst the ups and downs and pressures of a long and successful career as a writer/producer, culminating in being appointed an Adjunct Professor and featuring in the New Years Honours List, recognized by Her Majesty Queen Elizabeth II for services to television.

# The Tribe: A New World

## by

## A.J. Penn

*The official story continues in this novel, set immediately after the conclusion of season 5 of The Tribe television series, with The Tribe: A New World effectively becoming Season 6 in the continuing saga.*

Forced to flee the city in their homeland - along with abandoning their dream of building a better world from the ashes of the old - the Mall Rats embark upon a perilous journey of discovery into the unknown.

Cast adrift, few could have foreseen the dangers that lay in store. What is the secret surrounding the Jzhao Li? Will they unravel the mysteries of The Collective? Let alone overcome the many challenges and obstacles they encounter as they battle the forces of mother nature, unexpected adversaries, and at times, even themselves? Above all, can they build a new world in their own images - by keeping their dream alive?

# The Tribe: A New Dawn

## by

## A.J. Penn

*Following the many challenges in the best selling novel, 'The Tribe: A New World', the Mall Rats find themselves faced with an even greater struggle as they try to unravel the many unexplained mysteries they now encounter - in the equivalent of Season 7 in the continuing saga.*

What was the real mission of the United Nations survival fleet? Who is the enigmatic leader of the Collective? What really did occur at Arthurs Air Force Base? Is there something more sinister to the secrets revealed on the paradise island where they are now stranded?

Forced to resolve the agonizing conflict in their personal lives, the Mall Rats must also decide which path to take and whether or not to confront the ghosts of their past in their battle to survive against an ominous adversary. With the very real threat of human existence becoming extinct, can they endure against all odds to secure a future and the promise of a better tomorrow? Or will they suffer the same fate as the adults who had gone before and perish?

The tribe must fight not only for their lives but face their greatest fears to prevent the new world plunging further into darkness - and ensure hope prevails in a new dawn. And that they keep their dream alive.

# The Tribe: (R)Evolution

## by

## A.J. Penn

*In the sequel to the acclaimed best selling, 'The Tribe: A New Dawn' and 'The Tribe: A New World', 'The Tribe: (R)Evolution' is the third novel in the long awaited continuing saga based upon the cult television series 'The Tribe'.*

What secrets lay hidden in the ominous Eagle Mountain? Who are The Collective? And will the identity of their enigmatic leader be revealed?

Where is safe if invaders of faraway lands, intent on expanding their empire and fracturing alliances of all those struggling to rebuild and survive, ruthlessly pursue their own vision for the future and quest to gain domination and absolute power?

How does The Broker and The Selector fit into all the mystery surrounding Project Eden? Does anyone survive The Cube and the nightmarish Void?

Can the Mall Rats overcome all the unbearable challenges and obstacles they encounter to build a new and better world from the ashes of the old? Will they conquer their adversaries and ever recover from the heartache and agonising conflicts they experience in their personal lives?

Facing the very real threat of human extinction - can they endure? Adapt? Evolve? Survive? And keep their dream alive?

# The Tribe: Birth Of The Mall Rats

## by

## Harry Duffin

*The Birth of The Mall Rats is the first story in a compelling series of novelizations of the global cult television phenomenon, The Tribe.*

The world began without the human race. Now, after a mysterious pandemic decimates the entire adult population, it looks as if it will end exactly the same way. Unless the young survivors – who band together in warring Tribes – overcome the power struggles, dangers and unexpected challenges in a lawless dystopian society to unite and build a new world from the ashes of the old.

Creating a new world in their own image – whatever that image might be…

# FOR MORE INFORMATION

*Please visit the official website*

**www.tribeworld.com**

**"Like"**
**on**

**facebook.com/thetribeofficial**

**twitter.com/thetribeseries**

**instagram.com/thetribetvseries**

**youtube.com/thetribetvseries**

**vimeo.com/cloud9screenent/vod_pages**